Printing digital type
on the hand-operated flatbed cylinder press

Printing digital type
on the hand-operated flatbed cylinder press

by Gerald Lange

CHATWIN BOOKS
SEATTLE

ISBN: 978-1-63398-070-9

The author, editors, and publishers wish to extend their thanks to Bradley Hutchison, Paul Moxon, and Harold Kyle.

Trademarked names appear throughout this publication. Rather than list the names and entities that own the trademarks, or insert a trademark symbol with each mention of the trademarked name, the publisher states that it is using the names only for editorial purposes and to the benefit of the trademark owner, with no intention of infringing upon said trademark. Specifications of products are based on manufacturers' literature.

Contents

Part I: Overview

Introduction

You are reading this book because you are trying to create something. Our goals for this new edition are simple: we want to help you do just that. When you start work on your next project, we want to help you make it the best it can be. To show you what to look for when you choose the *right* type for all occasions. To give some perspective about the relationship between metal type and digital type on a polymer plate. To understand the real difference between different types of polymer plates and bases and to choose the best medium for your expression. To get your press set up for success, to think about ink, and to know what to do if things don't go quite right at first.

The four prior editions of this work have been useful to thousands of students and practitioners of letterpress printing at every level—including the editors. Over the years, this book has on many occasions prevented me wasting a great deal of paper, plates, ink, money, and time. My projects have included more creation and less frustration, and most importantly yielded better work at the end. All thanks to one little volume.

Almost thirty years ago, during our joint work on the 1989 exhibition catalogue for the Alliance for Contemporary Books Arts, called *A Southern California Decade,* I briefly introduced the author to digital type. The effect was immediate, as he began to talk about the potential that this, then-new, typographic medium could bring to his letterpress work, and that of his students at the University of Southern California, where he was teaching book arts at the time. In 1991 I commissioned his first experiments with letterpress printing from photopolymer plates generated from digital type. These were two broadsides with characteristics difficult or impossible to produce with metal type: Lee Hickman's *Anaximander,* and Lindsay Hill's *Songs I Learned.*

That brief introduction to the possibilities of digital type was the only thing I've ever been able to teach Gerald Lange—all the other lessons in the past thirty-plus years have been the other way. His approach to teaching is reflected in the philosophy that is the foundation of this book: being able to *do* is good, but being able to both do and *understand* is better. The sections of the book that deal with the evolution of digital type, how that evolution pertains to letterpress, and the account of the history of polymer plates provide context which may prove to be of as much practical help to your work as the hands-on instruction.

We're so pleased to be able to help share his teachings with a new audience. We hope you do good work and have fun doing it, and that this book helps.

Phil Bevis, editor

1. A Brief History of Photopolymer Plates

Printing with photopolymer plates is a relatively new phenomenon in the studio-letterpress world. Although commonplace in the industry since its introduction in the early 1960s, this was a technique that was rarely used by fine press printers. Mechanically produced plates of any kind were considered inadequate for reproducing typographic settings with the consistent quality of metal type, which until about the mid to late 1980s was still readily available.

The first noted practitioner of this process was San Francisco letterpress printer Julie Holcomb, who began using photopolymer plates with Bunting *flatbases* in the late 1980s to produce work for her graphic design clients. Subsequently, Los Angeles printer Patrick Reagh developed an economical magnetic base marketed as adjunct to his photopolymer plate processing business. At about this same time, James Trissel of The Press at Colorado College began experiments in relief printing with photopolymer and, with the assistance of a grant from the National Endowment for the Humanities, familiarized the fine press community with the process. However it wasn't until 1992, when publisher W. Thomas Taylor began printing his influential book arts review, *Bookways*, from digital type and photopolymer plates, rather than from Monotype machine composition, that the process was seen to have proven itself.

Printing digital type with photopolymer plates originally caught on because of an unlikely coincidence. As metal type resources were drying up, with closures of type foundries and typecasting operations all over the world, two somewhat unrelated technologies were fitted together as an alternative. In the 1980s the platemaking industry began to introduce water-based washout capability for processing plates along with technical improvements in the manufacturing of sheet photopolymer. Combined with the ready availability of precision magnetic registration systems (flatbases) and compact platemaking machines, this development roughly coincided with the evolution of professional typographic tools and high quality digital type for desktop publishing applications.

The new process was not only an acceptable replacement for metal type, it was the key to the survival of studio-letterpress printing, an activity that only a few years prior seemed doomed to extinction. Strangely enough, in recent years a resurgence of interest in letter-press has dramatically expanded the practice, and the majority of these new practitioners, armed only with computer and printing press, accept the photopolymer plate process as almost a matter of course. This influx of new entries to the field is fueled by educational institutions and community-based instructional facilities that in-creasingly focus on the process because of its cost-effectiveness and the ease with which it facilitates teaching.

With a photopolymer platemaking machine, plates can be made right in the studio from imaging initially created on a computer. This convenience gives the printer a degree of control not known since the era of the *Monotype composition machine*. Unlike the chemical waste generated in the processing of metals, water-soluble polymer waste (consisting of carbon in organic compounds) is safely flushed away. Environmental concerns that plague the photoengrav-er are not an issue in the processing of photopolymer plates.

Digital typesetting gives photopolymer plates an additional ad-vantage over metal type. Much of the drudgery associated with the composition of metal type is eliminated on the computer, which can accomplish this task with great speed, flexibility, and ease. With photopolymer plates there are none of the unique presswork problems common with metal type, such as *workups* or extensive *makeready*. If the plates are made properly, there are no worn or broken characters or possibility of running "*out of sorts.*"

Digital font character sets can be quite comprehensive as well, and there is no need to accumulate cabinets of type cases to accommodate the variances of size and style for a typeface. Using polymer plates can thus eliminate the spatial and organizational requirements demanded in maintaining a collection of metal type. Even in a fully equipped studio, platemaking equipment and a computer take up very little room. For some, removing lead from their work area or home-based studio is also a consideration.

When used with an appropriate flatbase registration system, photopolymer plates provide superior letterpress printing capabilities. They have exceptionally high *ink acceptance* and *ink transfer* qualities, a resilient and perfectly planar printing surface, and significantly eliminate makeready concerns. They reproduce, with exacting fidelity, digital imaging from high-resolution film and direct-to-plate technology. Sheet photopolymer plates are dimensionally stable and resistant to expansion or shrinkage during processing. Under optimal printing conditions photopolymer plates can reproduce fine lines accurately at .0015", *halftones* at 150 to 200 *dpi*, and isolated dots .0075" in diameter. They render letterforms with precision, provide outstanding coverage on solids and reverses, and have extraordinary wear characteristics (high resistance to abrasion).

The "desktop publishing revolution" was born on Super Bowl Sunday, 1984, with the Ridley Scott-directed commercial which introduced the Apple Macintosh personal computer to the world. This first successful application of the Xerox Palo Alto Research Center's graphical user interface brought with it the new phenomenon of the digital "font." PARC innovations also led to the development of the laser printer, the PostScript page-description language, and page-layout software (as well as many of the initial technical developments associated with the personal computer)—all of which laid the groundwork for a technology that would reconfigure the printing and publishing worlds.

Evolving from its toy-like infancy, desktop digital type became increasingly sophisticated. In 1989, it graduated to professional stat-

ure when Adobe Systems introduced its classically inspired Adobe
Originals series of typefaces complete with supplementary Expert
fonts containing additional character sets of small caps, oldstyle figures, alternate characters, and ornaments—typographic amenities
that had not been seen since the years of machine composition.

To add a flourish, like typefounders of the distant past, Adobe began
issuing distinguished type specimen booklets to accompany its font
releases. Quality type ceased to be the sole dominion of the proprietary computer systems previously used by commercial typesetters;
anyone with a personal computer could compose and design, and
print and publish whatever they chose. And design they did, often
without the benefit of any formal instruction or training.

It is possible to do typographic work without formal training or any
grounding in traditional methods or typographic history. However,
**an increasing number of leading digital designers have found
an awareness of our typographic heritage to be extremely ben-
eficial to the quality of their work.** Both type designer Matthew
Carter and innovative designer April Greiman (well-known figures
in the graphic design world, albeit of antithetical philosophies and
differing experiential backgrounds) have independently commented
that **the very best way to become accomplished at typographic
composition on the computer is to go back to the basics—to
first learn the handsetting of metal type.**

The technical restrictions that metal type imposes on the compositor (simply by nature of its physicality) are eliminated on the
computer. Consequently it can be difficult for the neophyte to com-
prehend the need for or benefits of self-imposed discipline. While
the structural characteristics and terminology associated with metal
typography remain embedded in digital technology, the rationale
for the procedural application of traditional typographic principles
seems meaningless within the confines of the computer screen. **The
lack of linear structure in the digital environment provides**

the user freedom of choice without knowledge of the quality of that choice.

The computer allows any user the ability to publish a newsletter, play a game of chess, or even design a typeface. But it is only commonly those with editing and publishing experience, or who understand the strategy of chess moves, or letterform structure, who will excel in these activities. **The computer can be a faithful servant, but it serves best only those who have knowledge of traditional techniques.**

With the viability of the process secured by technological advances, twentieth century developments have greatly multiplied the number of practitioners in studio letterpress. Harold Kyle's affordable and practical *Boxcar Base*, which used a polyester-backed plate and film adhesive drawn from the flexographic industry, was primary.

For many years letterpress printing had been a dying craft supported by a dwindling supplier base. Press manufacturers, type foundries, and specialty paper mills were closing. But then a number of factors contributed to this revival. Among these were increased interest from designers and marketers, and an influx of fresh practitioners from a non-traditional demographic.

Celebrity design maven Martha Stewart's proclamation that letterpress printing was proper etiquette for the production of wedding invitations was hugely influential in increasing consumer awareness and demand. Together with other leading design trendsetters, her promotion of letterpress in the media has contributed to a change in how letterpress products are perceived—from an obsolete production method to an aspirational luxury good.

In addition, an increased awareness developed on the part of print and product designers of the possibilities of letterpress printing. Marketing firms used the unique attributes and appeal of letterpress-printed items to distinguish their branding and campaigns.

The result of this (and other factors) was a growing consumer market, which encouraged a myriad of new entrants into an increasingly profitable niche.

During this period, there were changes beyond technology and demand—the profile of people working in the field. Up to the 1980s, letterpress printing was traditionally a male-dominated field. This unprecedented new generation of artists and artisanal printers opening studios and print shops were predominantly women.

Other promising, if not so fulfilling, developments have occurred in the printing industry. The availability of high-resolution laser printers utilizing toner-based film and filmless direct-to-plate technologies began to be available following the turn of the century. These, unfortunately, are not focused toward letterpress requirements, and do not yet meet specifications.

Part II: Photopolymer Plates

2. Technical Aspects of Photopolymer Printing Plates

Before you start setting type to make a photopolymer plate, you can help make the experience easier by examining one (or more) existing plates and looking at its different elements, and where possible comparing the plate to the finished work. Seeing the choices that experienced printers make, and the results they get, can be a great help.

Sheet photopolymer consists of a sandwich of four materials.
A support base of aluminum, polyester, or steel is bonded by an adhesive and *anti-halation* material to a layer of photosensitive nylon resin covered with a protective polyester film. Exposure of ultraviolet light to water-soluble photopolymer causes a chemical reaction that reforms and cross-links the polymer molecules and alters their solubility. Unexposed areas of the polymer retain their solubility. When an image is exposed on a photopolymer plate through a negative, and the plate is treated with water, the unexposed areas will wash away leaving the exposed image as a printing surface. Exposure rates have a range of latitude, and this variance can be controlled to encourage or halt the photopolymerization process. Different kinds of imaging—type, solids, halftones, fine lines—require different exposure times.

Where do polymer plates come from? Several firms have manufactured photopolymer plates. Over the years, well-known brands have included Jet, Miraclon, Nyloprint (BASF), and Printight (Toyobo). Plate stock is made in some 200+ configurations but only a small number of these are applicable to letterpress operations. **The most commonly used configurations have plate thicknesses at .037" to .039" (thin plates) or .057" to .060" (thick plates), with relief depths at .026" to .029" or .038" to .048",** and *hardness readings* at D 60° to D 85°. Any of these variations can affect the length of exposure, washout, drying, and curing times. For example, thick plates require longer exposure, washout, and drying times than thin plates.

A relief depth of .026" is all that is required for a cylinder proof press.

Although it is counterintuitive to many beginners, the shallower the relief depth the more image fidelity actually improves. This has to do with structural issues relating to the optimal thickness of sheet photopolymer. A deeper relief depth, such as .048", is suggested for platen presses (such as a C&P or Kluge) where ink run-off may be of concern due to truck, rail, or roller height variance. But even for debossing or foil stamping a relief thickness of .026" is quite adequate. **Before buying a flatbase it is best to discuss with a plate processor or printer experienced with polymer plates the various options available and the best configurations for the work intended** (see Chapter 13).

Common sense might dictate that the harder the plate the better, but as in the case of relief depth this is not necessarily the case. Hardness rating variations are based on a number of factors, including application, *substrate*, etc., but are most importantly related to *ink film acceptance* and transfer.

3. Photopolymer Platemaking Equipment

Many printers work only with plates they make themselves, many printers work only with finished plates supplied by firms like Boxcar, and others make a portion of the plates they use while ordering the rest, depending on the nature and scope of the project. Even if you never plan to make a polymer plate, knowing how and with what they are made can only help.

Photopolymer platemaking equipment provides for the ultraviolet exposure, washout, drying, and curing (post-exposure) of photopolymer plates. These separate processes are often combined as units in one machine though some manufacturers provide separate units. Photopolymer platemaking equipment requires water source and drainage hookups, enhanced electrical connections, and some form of shielding from dust and ultraviolet light, such as a darkroom.

While a darkroom itself is not a necessity, note that photopolymer plates will be fully exposed in a short period of time by direct sunlight. Fluorescent lamps used as working lighting should be covered with clear ultraviolet shields. Windows and skylights should be fitted with ultraviolet filters. Although some manufacturers suggest that photopolymer plates can remain in ambient light (incandescent lighting or indirect sunlight) for short periods of time without photopolymerization occurring, photopolymer plate stock must be stored in an area completely free from ultraviolet light exposure over time.

A platemaking machine is not the only way to expose, washout, dry, or cure photopolymer plates. **Platemaking machines are not that complicated and do not vary significantly from one manufacturer to the next. They are essentially an orderly, systematic, and precise method for processing plates.** At a basic level, plates can be exposed by any delivery mechanism that provides ultraviolet light, including chemical or ultra high-pressure mercury lamps, or by leaving them out in the sun. They can be washed out with a soft brush in the sink and dried with a hair dryer or even in an oven. This is perfectly fine for experimenting with images created as a result of direct manipulation of the photopolymerization process, but it cannot yield predictable results for reproducing type or images with consistent accuracy and precision.

While it might make economical sense to acquire just an exposing unit and forgo washout and dryer units, utilizing sink, brush, and hair dryer to cut costs, the washing out process in particular is crucial for consistent results. The ratio of good to bad plates is substantially lower when this step is not controlled in a mechanical manner and the cost of ruined plates and wasted labor will eventually negate any economic savings.

Platemaking machines are available from a number of manufacturers and distributors, such as Anderson & Vreeland, BASF, Jet, and Interflex. **Since this equipment is not inexpensive it pays to compare the literature and visit photopolymer plate processors who use the machine of interest.** Used platemaking machines are often available at a greatly reduced cost, but with an accompanying number of concerns. Make sure the platemaker was manufactured for processing photopolymer plates; many are not. If possible, try and see the machine in operation. There are routine maintenance replacements for any machine, primarily exposure lamps, brushes, and if the unit has had significant operational years, ballasts. Assume you will likely have to replace these items, and note that they are not inexpensive. Ensure that replacement parts are still available for the model, and try to obtain an operation and parts manual; if not, you may just end up with a nonfunctional machine.

4. Pre-Digital Typesetting Cautions and Considerations

In working through a job on the computer, think along traditional lines in work sequencing. **Word processing software should be used for the editing of text; page-layout software for design, typography, and layout; and illustration or image-editing software to create or refine illustrations.** Word processing programs should not be used for final output to an imagesetter. They do not have the sophisticated typographic capabilities of page-layout programs like enhanced *tracking* and *kerning*, and composition will suffer as a result. On the other hand, all text editing should be completed in a word processing program before it is imported to a page-layout program.

While simple editorial corrections can be made in page-layout programs, they are no match for the complex kind of editorial work that can be accomplished quickly and thoroughly in a word processing program. The reason for stressing word processing and page-layout software as a two-step process is that once a photopolymer plate is made, there is no second chance to make corrections. Going through the entire process again is the only way errors can be rectified—making the corrections on the computer, generating the negative, and processing another plate. In addition to costs for film and plates, rework can interrupt workflow and delay a project significantly.

When setting type on the computer it should be as if setting type by hand. If punctuation is normally hung into the margins, character combinations are kern-sawed, or small caps are carefully thin spaced when setting type in the stick, then the equivalent of these techniques should be applied on the computer. Given the professional state of page-layout programs such as Adobe InDesign or QuarkXPress, typographic composition need not be any different on a computer than it would be without it. The sophisticated capabilities, incredible flexibility, and speed of such software not only provides for instantaneous alterations, with careful application of compositional standards, it allows for greatly improved work, far beyond the inherent restrictions of metal type.

Page-layout programs often require preliminary adjustments as their defaults are in place for other concerns. It is necessary to zero-out automatic letter-spacing (tracking) or variance will be applied to your settings. Word spacing (±) variance, on the other hand, should be adjusted manually on a per font/per size/per line length basis. The defaults are usually found in the dialogue boxes that define "paragraph" attributes.

Editor's note: The ease with which type can be modified with digital programs sometimes leads to instances where finished work includes either use of the wrong type, or use of modified type that should not have been altered. If you know or think you might be using, as an example, bold italic, it is generally better to choose a professional font that includes that variation than it is to change the axis on a Roman font and thicken it up. Some of the people who view your finished work will be able to recognize your choices, and may hold strongly negative views about this practice. And even if you like the results in the moment, over time your views may evolve, and you may later wish you had spent the time to choose a typeface more appropriate to your project.

5. Film Negatives and Imaging

To convert computer imaging to photopolymer plates, files are output as film negatives with a high-resolution imageset- ter, such as a Linotronic. Service bureaus, photoengravers, and the like provide film negatives, and some photopolymer plate proces- sors provide them as well. Imagesetters are capable of output to film negatives at 2400 to 4800 dpi. A minimum final output of 2400 dpi is necessary to avoid *bitmapping* of type and images. The higher the resolution, the truer the imaging; type looks crisper and the stress and weight differences of the letterforms are more apparent to the eye. Proof your imaging with a laser printer at 600 dpi to get an idea of how it will actually look when you print it on your press.

Black and white *raster imaging* needs a minimum file resolution of 1200 dpi; grayscale images need a minimum file resolution of one- and-a-half to two times the final halftone line screen, e.g., 150 *lpi* requires 225–300 dpi. Prevent bitmapping of line art by converting raster images from grayscale mode to B/W bitmap mode at 50% threshold (in Adobe Photoshop) and ensure that vector images are set at 100% CMYK black in the color palette (in Adobe Illustrator). When additional elements are involved, such as type, export line art to a page-layout program (e.g., Adobe InDesign) for final output. **Note that illustration or image-editing software is not as well equipped as a page-layout program for the composition of type.**

Unless integral to the design, group imaging for the film negative in the following manner. Halftones should be separated from text or text separated from line work as these elements may need separate processing for best results. Carefully align imaging to minimize waste when film and plate are cut to size.

The required negative material is a matte-base lithographic film with discernible contrast between the matte and glossy sides. Film negatives are processed right reading and emulsion side up (RREU) to avoid contact problems during exposure of the photopolymer plate. The *emulsion side* sticks to the photopolymer surface (a matte surface facilitates proper vacuum drawdown, thus achieving full surface contact with the plate). Film negatives need a minimum density of 3.5 to 4.0 (preferably the latter) over the opaque areas (to prevent burn-through during exposure and loss of relief depth) and a maximum density of .05 at transparency (to ensure image clarity). There are industry developments, as well as experimental techniques, with toner-based film transparencies produced from laser or inkjet printers, but these do not quite meet the specifications required for high-end letterpress work.

Film negatives sent to a photopolymer plate processor should be free of chemical residue, surface dirt, smudges, scratches, and kinks. These can either reproduce on the plate or result in out-of-contact spots. Any opaque marking or masking should be on the film's glossy side. When shipping negatives, also provide same-size printed paper proofs (or PDF if sent online) with instructions as to finished plate size, registration guide needs (crop marks, alignment rule), and other requirements in regard to differing element forms, halftones, solids, and so forth. **Inspect film negatives carefully; what you see is what you get.**

Some photopolymer plate processors make film negatives in house without charge, but retain the material as proprietary. The elimination of this step does not allow for inspection of the negatives, so imaging must be carefully scrutinized for errors before it is transmitted. E-files should be sent in either EPS or PDF formats. For the latter, select Press Quality (configured for imagesetter output) in the corresponding Export option box.

6. The Platemaking Process—Preparation, Exposure

The basic process of making plates is fairly simple and routine, yet there are so many variances at each step that it is difficult to provide a specific procedure that will work on a consistent basis. Manufacturers of photopolymer plate stock and photopolymer platemaking equipment have procedural strategies that vary markedly from one to another. If you intend to process plates yourself, follow the steps suggested by the manufacturers of your equipment and stock. Accept the frustrations of trial and error and pay strict attention to the smallest details. Keep a journal with notes on your settings and results and eventually you will find consistent strategies that work best for you.

The first step is to inspect the film negative as they scratch easily and readily attract dust. Dirty negatives can be cleaned with certain solvents made for that purpose, but avoid excessive abrasion. Film negatives with kinks or scratches on imaging should be remade. Kinked areas, known as *cat winks*, may not seal properly and can cause image distortion; scratches may reproduce. Trim negatives with paper shears to the edge of the desired image, leaving a margin of about a quarter to half an inch. Brush the negative with an antistatic brush (Grumbacher makes quality brushes for use in the graphic arts industry) and spray with compressed air.

Raw photopolymer plate material must be brought to room temperature prior to processing as exposure times can be thrown off if plate material is processed when below 68°F. Cut the raw photopolymer plate to size in an area absent of ultraviolet light (sunlight/fluorescent lamps). Steel-backed plates can be cut with paper shears (or even tin snips), but a heavy-duty shears with built-in clamp, such as a Kutrimmer, is preferable. The clamp prevents the plate from shifting during the cutting process and facilitates final trimming. Polyester-backed plates are easily cut and trimmed with a paper shears or scissors.

Place the plate on the machine's vacuum frame and remove its protective film cover. Lift the film back in a smooth, continuous motion while keeping the plate lying perfectly flat. Never bend or flex a raw plate once the cover is removed. Position the negative on the plate with its emulsion side (dull or matte side) down. To ensure vacuum seal, the negative should not overlap the edges of the plate. Double check to make sure the imaging is *backward reading*.

A sheet of .004" *Kreene* cut to fit the full width and length of the vacuum table is then drawn down over the plate and negative, taking care not to disturb the negative's position on the plate. Do not use a transparent medium to ensure contact between negative and plate emulsion; this encourages light refraction and your imaging will suffer from distortion. Take extreme care to remove any dust particles (or hair) that may be clinging to the vacuum sheet. Spray out the vacuum unit with compressed air before and after the procedure. Clean the Kreene when necessary with distilled water (or rubbing alcohol) and replace it when dirty or when it fails to lay properly. On occasion, also blow out the vacuum plate's etched grid lines and suction holes to ensure optimal operation.

With the vacuum turned on, take a photographer's squeegee, acetate roller, or antistatic cloth, and move it across the entire surface of the sheet to ensure that there are no wrinkles or air spots trapped underneath. If you cannot obtain a proper seal (the vacuum gauge needle will wobble or surge between readings or you hear a slight hissing sound), redo the entire procedure. Without a proper seal, the negative and plate may not be in contact and exposure can result in imaging that is distorted or blurred. Some processors suggest covering the edges of the plate and negative with bleeder strips of Rubylith or scrap negative film. The strips are cut about an inch or so wide, a bit longer than width and length of the plate, and positioned to overlap the negative and the edge of the plate. Check carefully before exposing to make sure that these strips have not accidentally slipped onto your imaging. Avoid unnecessarily *ganging* plates as the vacuum seal is then less stable and could let go, with the result that all plates under exposure are ruined. Long pieces of 6- to 18-point brass or lead printer's rule, placed along the edges of the vacuum sheet, will doubly ensure that it is not disturbed during exposure. When vacuum is assured check the Kreene's surface to detect if dirt particles are clinging to the negative or the plate beneath it. These will show as tiny bumps. If they cover or are in near proximity to imaging you will need to stop the procedure and remove the particles before continuing.

Allow lamps to warm up by running them through a short exposure cycle prior to exposing plates. Depending upon the image and exposing source, exposure time can vary from three to six minutes. Fine lines require a longer exposure time than type while deep reverses require a shorter exposure. Halftones are generally exposed longer than type. **A 21-step gray scale** (from Dainippon or Stouffer) **is used to determine exposure rates** (most plate manufacturers supply an information sheet that provides the correct step when exposing their plates). The scale is used to test lamp intensity, which should be undertaken periodically as over time the exposure lamps degenerate and need to be replaced (at approximately 750 to 1,000 usage hours). If not, exposure consistency will wane with the consequence that plates are no longer able to hold fine detail. To compensate, exposure times need to be increased. Periodically, take a visual check of the lamps (during a short test exposure) to ensure that all lamps are functioning properly; use protective eye gear during this procedure as intense ultraviolet radiation can burn the cornea and conjunctiva of the eye.

When processing plates with imaging that requires different exposure rates, a staggered exposure may be required. To expose one element of the negative longer than another, mask off the element that needs less exposure with an opaque material such as Rubylith. With the vacuum on and negative-to-plate contact secured, register and tape the mask to the Kreene. After exposing the element that requires the longest exposure, remove the mask and continue to expose the entirety of the plate. Leave the vacuum on during this procedure. Determine the initial exposure rate by subtracting the rate of exposure of the shortest exposure requirement from that of the longest. **Do not make these or other changes nor open the exposure unit or otherwise interrupt the process while the lamps are turned on.**

7. The Platemaking Process—Washout, Drying, Curing

After exposure, turn the vacuum off, roll the Kreene back, remove the film negative, and attach the plate to the unit's platen (the upper plate that closes down, clamshell style, to the *agitator*). The soluble polymer remaining in the plate is then washed out in the bath. Washout units immerse the plate and agitate its surface with a motorized brush plate, plush pad, or ultrasound. Machines equipped for processing steel-backed plates usually have a sheet of magnetic rubber adhered to the platen to hold the plates securely in place during the washout process. Machines for processing polyester-backed plates have a sticky sheet of green PVC adhered to the platen. Some machines have a sticky sheet of magnetic rubber for processing both types of plates.

Machines with magnetic rubber sheeting platens can process polyester-backed plates with the addition of a detachable PVC carrier sheet (a carrier sheet can be fabricated by adhering PVC sheet adhesive to a thin sheet of non-corrosive steel—seal the edges with green die sealer or silicone caulk and coat the bottom with a water-based rust inhibitor followed by Lemon Pledge to prevent invasion and corrosion). If you routinely process significantly different thicknesses of plate material or use a detachable PVC carrier sheet, the brush should be adjusted to compensate. If this is the case, and your machine is not equipped with adjusters for this purpose, it will pay to work out a procedure with shims that can be inserted and removed, as too much pressure on the brush will damage the bristles.

The water level of the bath should be kept about a quarter of an inch above the brushes; if too low, plate surfaces will score. A cup of distilled white vinegar added to the bath (per seventeen gallons) will provide a bit of needed acidity and keep mineral deposits from accumulating. **Empty the bath water at the end of each day** to stave off fungi and prevent photopolymer waste from accumulating in the brush or the surfaces of the tank. Flush with fresh water. If removable, the brush plate should be drained while flushing the bath. The tank can be sprayed clean with a high pressure hose but take care not to spray the brush bristles or they will tangle and mat. Afterwards, rub the brushes slightly with the palm of your hand to spring the bristles upright. Leave the washout unit open overnight to allow them to completely dry out—on some machines the washout unit should never be closed down with the platen in contact with the brushes or the bristles will flatten and distort and eventually fail to make adequate contact with plates. Several equipment manufacturers suggest that brushes never be allowed to dry out. **Defer to your manual.**

Depending upon the machine and the manufacturer/brand and the thickness of the plate, **the recommended duration of washout and water temperature can range from 1 to 6 minutes at 59°F to 104°F.** Before washout, circulate the bath water to eliminate hot or cold spots and ensure an even temperature throughout. Too long a washout time will reduce image quality as polymerized areas may be undercut or their surfaces affected—small dots, fine lines, and serifs can easily disappear. A plate is properly washed out when the non-polymerized areas are completely removed to its *floor* (the plate's antihalation layer) and there is no evidence of undercutting. However, some thick plates may require a bit of residue left on the relief slope, at the plate's floor, to prevent undercutting at ends of lines or isolated dots.

While still adhered to the platen, the plate is thoroughly rinsed with a spray of fresh water from a high pressure hose to remove dissolved polymer materials and then dehydrated with a dampened sponge roller (or soft pad) to remove excess moisture. Check the plate at this time for surface defects and areas of faulty exposure. Remove unwanted exposed material that may have been created by scratches or pinholes in the film negative. Any such uncured polymer material left on the surface of the plate must be removed or it will harden in place.

The washed out plate is then put in the platemaking machine's dryer unit and dried at 122°F to 176°F for 5 to 25 minutes, depending upon the configuration of the plate material and machine. After drying, allow the plate to cool to room temperature and then post-expose it. Post-exposure cures the plate, stabilizing areas of halation and ensuring photopolymerization throughout the subsurface material. Plates can be post-exposed in the exposing unit or post-exposure unit on machines so equipped. **The vacuum is not needed during post-exposure, thus you can gang as many plates as possible—to reduce unnecessary aging of the lamps.**

The post-exposure rate is often the same length of time or longer than the initial exposure. A post-exposure time of one and a half to two times that of the main exposure time is usually recommended. When complete, remove the plate from the machine and trim unwanted unexposed material at the edges, cutting as perpendicular and parallel to the image as possible to facilitate initial alignment when placing the plate on the base. If using polyester-backed plates, adhere the film adhesive to the plate at this time.

8. Storage and Care of Photopolymer Plates

Raw plate stock must be protected from exposure to light (all visible light contains some ultraviolet light) and from non-linear pressure that could deform the sheet. Stock should be kept covered and in its original container, in a dustless area where environmental conditions are relatively constant (temperature should not exceed 77°F and humidity should not exceed 65%). Raw plate stock should not be used if older than a year from its date of manufacture. Cut pieces are especially vulnerable to environmental invasion at their edges. Different sized pieces should not be stacked one on top of another because of concerns regarding varied exposure accumulation and nonlinear pressure. Do not bend or flex raw plate stock. Avoid applying undue finger pressure while cutting stock as this can result in out-of-contact spotting.

Clean and pad dry previously printed plates before storage. Plates should be kept sealed in ziploc polyethylene bags and stored flat in a file drawer in an area free from exposure to light. Before closing the bag, blow a breath of air into it as the carbon dioxide and moisture will help ensure plate longevity (in photopolymer's early years, carbon dioxide storage units and baths were used to both protect raw stock and revive exposed plates). Ideally, storage temperature of stored plates should not exceed 100°F and humidity should be kept at 50 to 70%.

Do not leave previously printed plates lying around the studio. Photopolymer plates are vulnerable over time to ozone attack, with the severity of the damage increasing with rising temperatures. Ozone is thought to cause the cellular matrix to lose its resiliency and become brittle with the consequence that surface areas can crack and their edges crumble away during subsequent printing. Motors and other electrical devices generate ozone; thus photopolymer plates, both raw stock and finished material, should not be stored near them long term. The photopolymerization process itself can reduce the severity of ozone attack; hence longer post-exposure times to ensure proper curing may be a necessary caution (too long a post-exposure, however, can also contribute to a less resilient plate surface). Protection to lessen ozone damage (in severe conditions) involves treatment with antiozonant spray solutions, such as ArmorAll.

Contrary to popular suspicion, properly cured photopolymer plates will not dissolve when printing properly dampened paper. Exposing photosensitive polymer resin to ultraviolet light permanently alters its molecular structure, thereby rendering the polymer insoluble. Severe moisture damage (e.g., from rain or flooding), however, can cause the adhesive layer between photopolymer and backing to swell and erupt.

Part III: Printing

9. The Hand-Operated Flatbed Cylinder Proof Press

Unlike the iron handpress, which will not suffer a fool, the flatbed cylinder proof press welcomes all, novice to professional. Consequently, these presses have been indirectly responsible, since the mid 1970s, for the growth of the contemporary fine press community. The quality of the printed work produced on the hand-operated flatbed cylinder press can be as fine or as poor as on any other press; but its ease of operation, simplicity, and precision make it ideal for small-scale production. *[See also included article "Edition Printing on the Cylinder Proof Press," chapter 11.]*

For the majority of fine press printers the flatbed cylinder proof press, especially of Vandercook manufacture, replaced the iron handpress as the printing press of choice. The Vandercook SP (15, 20, 25) and Universal (I, III) presses (originally developed for laboratory testing in the late 1950s) have highly advanced inking and registration systems that make them ideal for precise edition work. These Vandercooks, along with the earlier model numbers 3, 4, and 219, greatly outsold all other similar reproduction proof presses and dominated the market. By 1962, over eighty percent of all cylinder proof presses in the US were Vandercooks.

As the result of renewed interest in studio-letterpress in the last decade, driven in large part by increased utility brought about by widespread access to and use of polymer plates, cylinder proof presses have become more sought after. Vandercooks in particular have become quite scarce and the used market price, which had been very stable, has risen dramatically. Because these presses have not been manufactured for several decades, Vandercook parts are increasingly hard to obtain. The remaining Vandercook parts inventory is held by NA Graphics, but many items are no longer available. It is next to impossible to find replacement parts for similar presses such as the Asbern or Challenge. It should be noted that the Swiss manufacturer of the highly regarded FAG cylinder proof press (which was discontinued in the mid 1970s) continues to supply refurbished presses that it acquires.

10. Notes on Press Operation and Maintenance

Your printing press is an invaluable tool; treat it accordingly.
Flatbed cylinder presses such as the Vandercook, Asbern, and Challenge are proof presses. As the following chapter will discuss, these presses were never meant for edition printing, but rather for single, perfect impressions which would then be used as repro proofs. Being outside the original design parameters, edition printing as a practice is extremely hard on the mechanical workings of these presses.

Negligence, even in small matters, such as failing to lubricate a press prior to use, will gradually take its toll. As will improper storage: the press should be covered when not in use to protect it from dust and its rubber rollers from ultraviolet light.

Use a high grade, non-detergent, SAE 20W machine oil for lubricating the press before each day's press run, making sure to wipe all moving parts with an oiled rag. Wipe a thin coat of silicone lubricating grease or oil on cylinder carriage bearing rails. Remove excess oil and grease from the press with a clean rag. Use Vaseline, not lubricating grease, on the vibrator's worm gear; this will prevent ink contamination in the event there is any spillage dripping down onto the rollers. (Vaseline can be used as an additive to thin out ink so it is potentially less damaging than oil or grease.) **If you hear a squeak** (an indication of neglect—the rider roller is often the first to complain) **or any unusual noise while operating the press, stop your work immediately and search for the cause.**

Common sense should prevail when working with a printing press of any kind. Avoid practices that cause extreme stress on the cylinder carriage bearings, such as die cutting, debossing, and scoring. This type of work is best left to platen presses. Once the bearing rails start showing wear or disintegrating, cylinder alignment and tracking are thrown off and your work will suffer for it. (Test the rails by wiping an oil soaked rag along their length. The surface of the cast iron is disintegrating if tiny sparkles of metal show on the rag.) Keep tools off the press bed and rails at all times, as you cannot effectively repair a damaged or scored cylinder or bed.

Do not work beyond the technical limits of a press by increasing the cylinder packing over factory specifications, or forcing the printing surface slightly above or below type high. This can happen easily enough if you are unsure of the height of your base and/or plate, or a printer might do this intentionally because of the configuration of a job, but disturbing the purposeful engineering and sync of a press can result in incorrect lay of ink on the printing surface, and slurring is the likely result.

In operation, it is advisable that cylinder movement be smooth and consistent and neither overly fast or slow as this can cause smudging of the inked form. Too fast a movement can also cause wear and damage to a press. When printing, the operator should in any case hold the sheet to be printed tight against the cylinder as it completes its rotation. This has the side benefit of keeping the movement at a correct speed. Likewise, do not "short roll" a cylinder press to increase speed of production as damage can result to the trip/print mechanism. **Always roll completely to the end of the press bed.**

Some folks believe a slow movement will impart *"dwell,"* as would be the case on an iron hand press during the action of pulling and releasing the press handle—it is a common assumption that if the handle is held back, the dwell before release allows the ink more time under pressure to penetrate the paper sheet (in historical practice, the press handle was pulled and released immediately). This is simply not true on a cylinder press. Unlike platen impression, a cylinder provides only a thin line of impression force as it travels the bed; halting or slowing this action can result in odd disturbances of inked image or type.

A paragraph by Joseph Moxon from his *Mechanick Exercises: Or, the Doctrine of Handy-works Applied to the Art of Printing* (1683–4) supplies a very perceptive understanding of hand presswork that is quite applicable today:

> He keeps a constant and methodical posture and gesture
> in every action of Pulling and Beating, which in a train
> of Work becomes habitual to him, and eases his Body,
> by not running into unnecessary diversions of Postures or
> Gestures in his Labour, and it eases his mind from much
> of its care, for the same causes have constantly the same
> effects. And a Pull of the same strength upon the same
> Form, with the same Beating, and with the same Blankets,
> &c. will give the same Colour and Impression.

11. Edition Printing on the Cylinder Proof Press

Excerpted from the author's "Edition Printing on the Cylinder Proof Press: A Historical Perspective," *Parenthesis: The Journal of the Fine Press Book Association*, Oxford, England. Number 3, May, 1999. Revised, with slight additions, editorial changes and footnotes not originally included in the article.

To my knowledge, the first documented use of a modern flatbed cylinder proof press for editioning a finely printed book was in the early 1950s at the newly formed Thistle Press. This was the Bert Clarke and David Way printing of volumes IV through XII of the Frick Collection catalogue (completed in 1955). John Dreyfus, in his book, *Bert Clarke, Typographer,* notes the pair abandoned the iron handpresses used to print the first three volumes of the catalogue (published in 1949), after having "successfully experimented with alternative methods for printing dampened handmade paper on a large Vandercook proof press."

It was not until the mid-1960s, however, that the hand-operated flatbed cylinder press began to be viewed by some printers as an ideal press for limited edition production work. The most notable early practitioner in this regard was Claire Van Vliet of the Janus Press. Her earliest work on a Vandercook proof press stems from the period of her apprenticeship (1958–1960) at John Anderson's The Pickering Press. Probably the most influential advocate of the hand-operated flatbed cylinder press, however, was Walter Hamady of The Perishable Press, Ltd., whose first printed work on a Vandercook appeared in 1966 when he began teaching at the University of Wisconsin-Madison.[1] Both Van Vliet and Hamady were (and are) first and foremost, artists, and practiced the printing arts with a different perspective than their predecessors. Their stylistic approach to personal bookmaking was to have a significant impact on the like-minded fine press "renascence" of the mid-1970s.

1   Interestingly, Van Vliet immediately preceded Hamady at Madison, teaching there for a year in 1965. Previous to this, according to the bibliographic evidence, Hamady printed on a clamshell platen press.

As the commercial printing industry completed its shift away from letterpress technology in the late 1960s and early 1970s, flatbed cylinder proof presses and other remnants of the metal type era were flooding into the used printing equipment market. Only a few years after Lewis Allen published his seminal *Printing With the Handpress* in 1969, the iron handpress, the subject of his study, was already losing its ground as the press of choice for a new generation of fine printers.[2] From William Morris to Allen, the iron handpress had remained the only machine deemed traditionally appropriate for hand edition work. Allen begrudgingly felt that a cylinder press could only be considered a legitimate handpress if the roller mechanism was removed (and the form inked by hand); his contemporary, Harry Duncan, thought that the addition of a tympan and frisket cage attached to the end of the bed would suffice. This standing defense of tradition was itself, ironically, a bit blind to traditional technique. In 1933, printing historian Paul Johnston lamented that the "modern" mechanical use of rollers to ink a form had irrevocably invalidated the virtue of, and the skills required for, "hand press printing" by dispensing with the difficult, but more touch-sensitive, ink balls.[3]

Despite the argument, the iron handpress was increasingly forsaken

2   In this book, Allen has written that Bruce Rogers was an early practitioner of printing on a Vandercook. I have been unable to find any evidence of this except to note that Rogers was associated with the Thistle Press and the Frick Collection catalogue and may have been influential in Clarke and Way's decision to complete the project with a Vandercook.

Further note: In a letter from William J. Murray, dated March 31, 2006, he notes that his acquaintance William G. Haynes worked on the Thistle Press Frick catalog for three years. Murray states "I distinctly remember his talking about the use of the Vandercooks in the printing and that the project was considered by the workmen to have been under the overall supervision of Bruce Rogers, who at his age (early 80s) did not want the day to day burdens of the printing project itself. But Bill Haynes remembered that he did come, but rarely, to the shop to look at the printing in progress. Haynes recalls meeting him there."

3   Rollers were first used as inking devices on printing presses in 1812.

for the very reasons Clarke and Way had abandoned it in the 1950s: efficiency and availability. In 1973, while beginning work on the Greenwood Press *Phaedrus*, printer Jack Stauffacher chose handset type and the Vandercook proof press as "the simplest and most trustworthy tools" for producing the book. As more and more of the fine printers entering the field took up the hand-operated flatbed cylinder press, resistance fell by the wayside. By 1980, in his lecture "The Technology of the Hand Press," Duncan referred with shielded optimism to the "upstart" cylinder press as "the new god."

Editor's note: Used respectfully and skillfully, a cylinder proof press can produce editions of beautiful work from either metal type or polymer plates. That same press, with lower quality type, plates, material, or improper preparation, can yield results best described as disappointing. The goal of this book is to help you produce the former, not the latter, with minimal wear on a press which, if treated properly, can continue to serve generations of printers to come.

12. Cylinder Packing and Makeready

Cylinder packing top blanket*s* (drawsheets), *under blankets*, and *undersheets* for various model Vandercooks are available from NA Graphics. A top blanket of .007" Mylar drawn over an under blanket of .021" Kimlon (a latex-impregnated paper made by Neenah Paper Co.) and one to four .006" manila undersheets will usually suffice. (A single piece top blanket and under blanket combination at .026" is still available for some models). The exact number of undersheets required for adequate packing is dependent upon the thickness of the paper to be printed. A Mylar top blanket and Kimlon under blanket provide a hard, resilient packing surface. Hard packing is required when printing photopolymer plates because of their exact planar surface and the uniform resilience of the photopolymer.

On a cylinder press there is no real need to "bury" makeready beneath the Mylar drawsheet. Pack the cylinder to within .002" to .005" of the desired impression and draw the packing as tightly and evenly as possible. If the Mylar begins to ripple across its surface when viewed in reflective light, back off a notch on the ratchet until the smooth sheen returns. *Proof* directly onto the Mylar for placement. Additional makeready taped to the Mylar should be in the form of overlays—.002" nonslip paper packing, .001" to .0015" high grade tracing paper, or .0005" silk tissue provide a useful variation range. Nonslip paper packing is manufactured in thicknesses ranging from .002" to .016". Try to have at least one overlay of nonslip paper packing to prevent the Mylar from burnishing the back of the printed sheet at points of impression. Keep the number of overlays to an absolute minimum.

Draw and stretch the overlay sheet tightly over the Mylar leaving an allowance of an inch or two beyond the printing paper size. The tape should be placed diagonally at each corner of the makeready and pulled taut. If the overlay slips slightly under finger pressure or bulges unevenly, reapply. For visual reference take another proof directly on your makeready and then wipe clean with fast drying type or plate wash. Additional pieces of carefully prepared makeready buried beneath the primary overlay will increase the impression at problematic areas of the form. These strips should be feathered at the edges to provide an even transition to the impression. Prevent the overlay packing from drawing down along the cylinder after repeated impression by tagging the sheet with pieces of tape at intervals along its top edge.

13. Flatbases

The only accouterment needed to print photopolymer plates, other than your existing printing equipment, is a flatbase. Photopolymer plates are mounted directly to bases made of wood, lead, Plexiglas, aluminum, zinc, and steel. Aluminum is preferable because of its molecular density, dimensional stability, and lighter weight. Photopolymer plates are manufactured with steel, polyester, or aluminum backing. Almost all printers working with photopolymer currently use magnetic or non-magnetic adhesive flatbases. Magnetic bases were developed first, followed by the non-magnetic adhesive kind.

Steel-backed plates are more often used in combination with magnetic bases. They are mounted simply by placing them on the base and can be quickly repositioned or removed. Most industry-grade flatbases are made of aluminum with magnetic inserts. There are several established manufacturers of these flatbases: Brüder Neumeister, Bunting Magnetics, Kocher + Beck, and T. D. Wright.

The purchase of a flatbase is a significant expense. Being informed about the attributes of each as they pertain to your requirements is essential. Both magnetic and non-magnetic bases have their proponents.

Magnetic:

The most well known magnetic flatbase is the Bunting Magnetic Cerface Flat Base. Bunting Magnetics began manufacturing magnetic flatbases in 1985; the Cerface model was introduced in 1994. The Cerface is made of precision ground aluminum flat stock with a gridded surface of ceramic magnet inlays. These bases are made in standard sizes ranging from 2 by 4 inches to 8-1/2 by 11-1/4 inches cast and machined to specific thicknesses (and can accommodate any press/plate configuration up to one inch thick, including galley proof presses sans bed plate or presses with non-standard type height requirements, such as foreign made presses). Custom size bases are available up to 19 by 39 inches. The magnetic inlays are resistant to solvents and abrasion, and their *shear strength* is substantial enough to resist *plate travel* in most letterpress printing work. The Cerface, like similar industry-grade flatbases, is quite expensive and represents a significant investment, thus it is only recommended for commercial or semi-commercial use where stable, precise registration, and consistency of impression are imperative. Registration devices, such as *pin registration* and scribe lines are optional additions. Bases can also be supplied in steel housings for specific operations, such as *embossing/debossing* and *die cutting*.

The Patmag (developed by the aforementioned Patrick Reagh) is an economical alternative. The Patmag is a flat stock of aluminum covered with a thin sheet of magnetized rubber (the same material, Magback, is used on the platen of platemaking machines to hold steel-backed plates during washout). While magnetic rubber sheeting is not as inflexible, magnetically strong, or durable as magnetic inlays, when it wears out or is damaged the manufacturer will replace it at nominal cost. These bases are made in standard sizes ranging from 3 by 4 inches to 12 by 16 inches.

Non-Magnetic or Adhesive:
Plates without steel backing are generally adhered to the base with glue or film adhesive. Flatbases specifically designed for such plates are the Boxcar Base from Boxcar Press (developed by Harold Kyle in 2000) and the Eluminum from Elum Designs (introduced in 2009). The bases are a precision ground flat stock of aluminum that uses transparent polyester-backed plate stock with film adhesive interlay (both supplied by the manufacturers). The bases come in two depth thicknesses, Standard and Deep Relief, to accommodate either thin (.038") or thick (.060") plates.

The most popular of the non-magnetic flatbases is the Boxcar Base, which has an *anodized* surface and quarter-inch grid and is available in standard sizes from 4-1/2 by 7-1/2 inches to 24 by 24 inches (the largest Deep Relief base is 13 by 19 inches). Custom larger size bases are available. The Eluminum has a colored anodized surface and laser-etched quarter-inch grid and is available in standard sizes from 4-1/2 by 7-1/2 inches to 9 by 12 inches. Both these bases and the Patmag are priced comparably, which has made them quite popular in the studio-letterpress community.

When ordering any base it is crucial to know the thickness of plate that will be used with it. **The proper configuration of a Cerface base is determined by subtracting the thickness of the photopolymer plate from type high (.918") or galley high (.968") *sans* galley.** Bunting does not recommend the use of underlays with its base. The Patmag is undercut to a standard thickness of .858", thus it can accommodate a .060" plate as well as thinner plates with appropriate underlay. A type-high gauge will accurately determine the correct thickness of underlay required when switching plate stock. Acetate underlay material can be purchased at graphic art supply stores in calibrated thicknesses. The Boxcar and Eluminum flatbases are .876" thick and, with film adhesive interlay measuring .004", allow for a plate thickness of .037" with .001" underlay (dependent upon variance in base thickness).

Since the height of the Cerface is warranted accurate between .000" and .001", these bases can be used in combination; thus the printer can buy one size and add as needed. Boxcar and Eluminum flatbases are similarly guaranteed accurate to .001" (±). The Cerface flatbase is also parallelized (parallel throughout the measure). With the Patmag, however, which has a tolerance between .001" and .003", it is better to purchase the largest size base that will fit the press bed rather than several smaller bases used in combination (in general this would be the most cautious approach). Too wide a variance in tolerance between bases is detrimental to accurate presswork. In determining the width and length of base(s) allow room in the press bed for lockup materials. If you are using a *platen press*, also allow for registration gauges and guides outside the surface area of the base.

14. Base lockup and Press Preparation

Before you lay your base in the bed of the press, wipe clean all contact surfaces. These include press bed, bottom and top of base, and bottom of photopolymer plate. Surround the base with wooden *furniture* or *reglets* to prevent scoring from the *quoins*. When tightening the quoins make sure that the base does not rise in the bed. Lock in position; a slight "snug" will do. Multiple bases must be locked up with extreme care to ensure that their surfaces are true to each other and underlaid to correct any imbalances.

Clean the surfaces of your base carefully with a lint free cloth to which you have applied press wash or mineral spirits. **Be extra careful in cleaning a rubber magnetic sheet base.** Any form of abrasion and/or solvent is going to remove minute material from its surface. Solvents are also invasive and can eventually deteriorate the bond or cause swelling. This caution also applies when cleaning plates that are adhered to flatbases with film adhesive. In some industrial applications, die sealer is recommended to prevent solvent invasion and/or ensure plate edge adhesion.

Editor's note: Remember that flatbases are made from aluminum, which is relatively soft and can be damaged by being dropped on a press bed or floor, by cylinder overpacking, by running a press with tools on the plate, by placing the plate on a press bed which has objects on it and then subjecting the flatbase to stress, or in any number of other ways generally stemming from carelessness. All of these can result in a flatbase which has high or low areas which will prove troublesome for future use, and will be expensive to replace.

15. Plate Registration

Two major problems to face in printing with photopolymer plates are registration and plate travel. Registration is extraordinarily difficult with photopolymer plates because of the lack of precise mechanical or visual reference for placement. Plates are usually out of register at an angle and there are no built-in horizontal or vertical references from which to correct this. On a cylinder press adjustment of paper guide knobs is initially not often adequate enough to correct this problem, especially if more than one plate has to be registered.

There have been a variety of sophisticated techniques developed to control these problems. Some printers have registration aids carefully introduced at various stages in the platemaking process. These include incorporating *keys* into the layout, plate positioning at exposure, template cutting after curing, and mounting guides on the base. If you are consistently working with standardized formats and press forms this approach makes good sense. Even with such aids, however, if the plate is still as much as a point out of register they amount to just so much wasted effort. **A simpler registration aid is the inclusion of a horizontal hairline rule about an inch or so outside of your design layout.** This is generated along with your other imaging and exposed together when making the plate. The rule serves as a printable reference line that is later removed with a blade once the plate is in register.

Registration begins simply by placing the plate in its approx-imate printing position on the base. The Bunting Cerface, Boxcar, and Eluminum bases facilitate this through visual reference to their grid, while Patmags do not. After a proof is taken, you can tell how far and in what direction the plate has to be moved and rotated. A steel-backed plate can be removed from a magnetized base by slipping a pad (tablet) knife under one of its corner edges and slowly lifting the plate while sliding the blade along under it. At some point the plate will resist the magnetism and pop up. Do this cautiously on a magnetized rubber-sheeting base, as it is quite easy to cut into and scar its surface.

When angular registration is off by only points, a plate's position can be refined without completely removing it from the base. Prevent the plate from slipping in a second direction (a side where it is in correct position) with a reference guide. A piece of discarded plate material, cut about the same length of the plate and butted up against the side of the plate will suffice. Then lay another piece of plate material down on the base, one edge at the desired reference line to which the plate has to move and the other edge butting up against the plate at an angle. Pick up the edge of the plate with the knife; when you can feel the plate is loose enough to slip but not to completely detach itself, drag the out-of-position edge to the reference plate you have laid down. If only a slight movement is necessary to correct the plate at an angle a brass bookbinder's pallet, or broad edge screwdriver and small hammer, can be used to nudge a small or medium size plate into position. With great care, position the tool against the corner edge of the steel floor of the plate and tap.

When working with a magnetic rubber sheeting base, once the plate is in register, outline its sides with a strip of white artist's tape (do not use masking tape as its edges can curl, pick up ink from the rollers, and transfer to your printed sheet) or outline the plate with a precision-point ink marker. This will allow you to monitor for plate travel. If the tape begins to buckle or the marking disappears, reposition.

The magnetic pull of a Cerface base is so strong it will often cause a plate to pull down hard to the base before you can get it into ap-proximate position. To eliminate this problem, **a plastic smooth-ing tool** (available in the paint department of hardware stores) **is an invaluable aid.** Sandwich the plate and the tool together with the plastic piece underneath. Lay them both down at an angle to the base, making contact first with the bottom edge of the plate. This will allow you some leverage. Move them together into position and then carefully draw out the tool. For finer adjustments, pick up the edge of the plate with the knife and insert the tool between the plate and the base only far enough to lift the plate but not so far as to break it completely from the base. Hold the tool and the plate together and push them to the reference guides. When in position, slowly pull out the insert.

The polyester-backed plates used on non-magnetic bases are adhered with film adhesive designed for use with photopolymer plates. The film adhesive has protective sheeting on both sides (sheets) or just the outer side (rolls). In the case of the former, one side is peeled off to attach to the plate and the other before attaching the plate to the base. The plates are easily picked up and positioned with the adhesive attached. The transparency of the plate facilitates lineup with the grid pattern. Be very careful to keep the protective sheeting in an area free of particulate matter, as you will need to reattach it once the plate has been removed from the base. One clear advantage of the transparent polyester-backed plate over the steel-backed plate is that once a plate is in register, elements of the imaging can be cut out with a sharp blade and then repositioned in place for subsequent press runs, which is very useful for spot color work.

Minute adjustments to plates slightly out of angle can and should be made with the press paper guides, but do not adjust them to the point at odds to one another where the paper sheet will be crossing over the cylinder at an angle, as this could throw registration off, especially if the sheet is long and narrow. Paper guides should initially be set in the mid of their adjustable range to give some latitude in later adjustment.

Plate travel is rarely encountered with Cerface flatbases, but it is a persistent demon on magnetic rubber sheeting bases.

Plate travel is obviously damaging to an edition run. The weaker the resistance to directional shear stress the more likely the possibility of travel. On a flatbed cylinder press with a fixed bed, plates tend to travel in a specific direction (toward the cylinder). The amount of surface printing area and the physical size of the plate also affect travel. **Halftones or illustrations with broad expanses of surface exposure tend to travel more than type. Small plates tend to travel more than large plates.**

A common way to eliminate travel on a Patmag is to lightly glue the plate to the magnetic surface with a non-permanent mounting adhesive, such as 3M's 75 Spray Adhesive. Once the plate is in position and its placement carefully marked, the plate is removed from the base and its bottom surface lightly sprayed with adhesive. Allow the adhesive to tack before repositioning; subsequent removal will be easier and less damaging to both the plate and the magnetic surface of the base. Plates can curl or distort and pieces of the magnetic surface can be torn out if the plate is adhered too securely. The amount of adhesive and duration of tacking required will vary with the physical size and amount of surface area of the plate.

Cautionary Notes:
As is the case with the Cerface, plate travel is rarely encountered with polyester-backed plates (used on flatbases like the Boxcar) due to the shear strength of the film adhesive supplied with them. Caution is recommended, however, when applying adhesive to avoid capturing air bubbles or stretching that can result in film caliber disturbance and irregularities. Bubbles are more common with film adhesives with a thick protective backing. Captured air bubbles must be removed with syringe or razor blade and then pressed flat or they can cause erratic impression spotting during printing. Lay the plate down to the base in an even rolling fashion to prevent buckling, especially if there are divergent elements to the imaging such as large solids—solids do tend to distort the level plane of polyester-backed plates and attention to lay down is advised. Keep

work areas clean as dirt and other debris can attach to film adhesive and contribute to further problems. Lifting and repositioning plates must be done carefully as the adhesive can stretch, detach, or curl and would need to be replaced. Film adhesives are not recommended for use with steel-backed plates, which could otherwise be used on a non-magnetic base, as the plates can bend or buckle when removed from the base.

16. Rollers and Inking

The combination of the right printing paper and ink, correct impression, proper ink viscosity, exacting roller height adjustment, and judicious inking will deter most problems encountered during press editioning.

First of all it is crucial that the rollers be kept in excellent working condition. Clean them thoroughly with press wash or mineral spirits after every run, using a soft open-weave cloth (such as surgical toweling) to pick up the solvent. Some roller manufacturers suggest that water-miscible roller washes, rather than petroleum distillates such as mineral spirits, be used to clean synthetic rubber compound rollers. Avoid household cleaners and cooking oils as these have been revealed to be detrimental to roller life and can gum up moving parts and cause rusting. **Once a week** (or between color shifts) **treat the rollers to a washup with an ink-glaze remover and rubber rejuvenator.** Avoid composition (glue/glycerin) rollers as they react badly to environmental conditions and will begin to lose their dimensional stability, eventually dissolving and dripping onto the press bed and ink drum. **Never leave rollers lying flat when off the press.** Use a roller rack to keep them round.

Rubber rollers react to inks, solvents, ultraviolet light, and other environmental conditions and over time will begin to swell and crack, especially at the ends. When this affects consistent edge-to-edge printing they should be replaced. Rubber rollers also harden with age as plasticizers, which act as binding agents, leach out. Vandercook recommended a durometer hardness reading not to exceed Shore A 20° and suggested monitoring roller hardness monthly. A hardness reading exceeding factory specifications was felt to result in "a poor lay of ink." On the other hand, a harder than normal durometer reading (Shore A 20°) is recommended when printing on photopolymer plates. Increase in roller hardness is less a consideration for replacement than edge swelling or surface damage.

Set roller height at a slightly higher reading than normal when printing photopolymer plates and constantly monitor it during the edition run to keep the rollers in exact position. Because the surface of a flatbase is quite near *type high,* rollers that are out of adjustment can "bottom" and transfer ink to plate floor or base surface. Rollers even slightly out of adjustment can deposit ink at the edges of plates and result in minute transfer of ink to the printing paper and, like workups associated with metal type forms, this may not be immediately detected.

This is such a common problem with photopolymer plates that a *frisket mask* is suggested as a preventive measure. The normal roller gauge setting recommended by Vandercook is an ink strike of 1/16 to 3/32 of an inch. Try to stay within a range of 1/32 to 1/16 of an inch especially at the preparatory stages of an edition run. This helps reduce the amount of ink deposited on the form and keeps the ink from hiding defects at the proofing stage. Due to press aging and roller swelling, however, roller settings may have to be altered. **Different typographic elements require different settings**. Halftones, rules, and short lines of type require higher settings; solids, large blocks of text, or large sizes of display type require lower settings.

Check the roller height setting (the press should be off impression—on trip) with the vibrator roller always in the same position in its travel back-and-forth on the worm gear. On most presses the vibrator will complete its travel right-to-left and left-to-right as it moves down the length of the bed—if you roll the cylinder carriage when the vibrator is at the operator's side of the press it will arrive at the opposite side when the carriage reaches the end of the bed. Pick a position and stick with it. Always take the roller height reading in the same area of the press bed. These practices will provide you with consistent reference. To ensure the accuracy of your adjustments bring the carriage back to the feedboard and then down again to the end of the press and verify your reading.

When you first ink up a press the ink is applied in a thin bead-like strip along the entire length of the rider (idler bar). At this point, you need only as much ink as is minimally required to cover the vibrator and ink drum. Once your rollers are adjusted, printing image is in position, and impression is exact, you can then begin to add enough ink to reach *edition state* (optimal ink film density). Afterward, ink is added to the rider in small amounts only in those areas where it is needed. Preventing progressive ink buildup requires constant diligence. Worked out ink needs to reach temperature stasis before applying it to the press. Ink should fully circulate on the rollers before beginning any printing.

There are times when ink should be removed from the press. The *form* should be cleaned when ink begins to spread beyond letterform printing surfaces. Ink is viscous and if not contained it will continue to attract additional ink from the rollers. If there is too much ink being transferred to the form it needs to be removed from the rollers. **To clean ink from the press during an edition run, work in the following order: rider, vibrator, ink drum.** If removing all the ink from the rider doesn't do the trick, remove all the ink from the vibrator, and so on. If ink has gone bad during a run, clean the entire roller set, allowing the rollers to completely dry out before re-inking.

To clean ink from printing surfaces, wipe with a fast drying type or plate wash applied with a tight-weave cloth (such as surgical sheeting) and dry with a spray of compressed air. Proof-up and, when back at the edition state, continue printing. Do not use slow drying solvents (such as mineral spirits) to clean ink from printing surfaces. There are commercial solvents specifically formulated for cleaning photopolymer plates, though any fast drying type wash will do the job. When cleaning photopolymer plates be careful not to wipe the form too harshly (pad, don't rub). While photopolymer can withstand a great deal of direct pressure with its surface areas remaining intact, isolated fine lines or serifs are easily damaged from abrasive side-to-side movement.

Ink bearers are often used on the iron handpress to facilitate the hand inking of type forms. With a flatbed cylinder press these are impractical. The cylinder carriage bearings and rails, being fixed in position, eliminate the need for ink bearers. On the other hand, an aging cylinder press is not true to its factory specifications and may not print evenly over the length or width of its bed. In this case roller supports can greatly ensure even inking. A pair of 18- to 24-pt point brass *barweld rule* cut to a length slightly shorter than the effective printing length of the press will serve this purpose well. The rule are placed next to the rails but separated from them with two pica widths of furniture. The supports are usually chamfered and rounded at the surface edge ends to prevent roller nicking. The Mylar tympan will have to be cut away where the supports come in contact with it, both to prevent wear to the supports but also because the supports will print to the tympan and accumulated ink could transfer to the paper during feeding. **Note also that ink can build up on both the tympan and the supports during a print run, gradually affecting roller height.**

Ink bearers are often set one or two points above type high to prevent the rollers from coming down too hard on the printing surface, but roller supports generally do not need this adjustment. Any adjustment in the form that is over type high will affect roller height, but occasionally a slip of .001" to .002" underlay at one end or the other of a roller support will serve to adjust irregularities in roller tracking. Sometimes a strip of underlay at one end or another of a base will also even out the inking. Roller supports can also be incorporated into imaging and printed as either part of the photopolymer plate or as strips alongside of it.

For efficient control during presswork, print different typographic elements (halftones, line art, solids, reverses, or even

different sizes of type) in separate runs. Do not mix different kinds of forms in your lockup—bases, metal type, engravings, etc. It is easier and often faster to print several relatively simple runs than to constantly monitor and struggle with a complicated form. **Keep it simple.** If your editions are 100 to 150 copies or less this makes good sense. When running longer editions it may pay to work out the complexities, but long edition runs on a hand-operated cylinder press will invariably reveal a printer's fatigue and neglect. **Break your run into sessions** with a washup, fresh ink, and new makeready to revitalize the work. It is counterproductive to try and do more than you can effectively control.

17. Notes on Ink and Paper

Ink is a major source of confusion, suspicion, and superstition, and no two printers seem to have the same opinion on the subject. Letterpress printers might want to take their cues from printmakers who seem to know their inks intimately. Finding the right ink is a matter of trial and error. Unfortunately, there is no one formulation that will satisfy the needs of every job.

Most contemporary inks are formulated to allow them to stay "open" on high-speed presses; consequently they are not well suited to printing on hand-operated presses. Stone lithographic inks are more appropriate. They have workup qualities suitable for hand applications as they are intended for printing at slower speeds. In this regard, Handschy's Crayon Black BK-8035 and Graphic Chemical & Ink's Lithographic Senefelder's Crayon Black No. 1803 have proved especially fine inks for general text printing.

Additives are often useful in altering the characteristics of ink, but be very cautious in their application; if you do not have to use them, don't. Common additives include magnesium carbonate for stiffening ink, and reducing varnishes for loosening ink. Lithographic roll up ink is also very useful for adjusting viscosity of stiff blacks. To accelerate drying on nonporous papers, cobalt dryer (an oxidizer) is quite useful. For full coverage of solids a product called Setswell Compound is invaluable, as it increases the surface flow of the ink. All of these inks and additives are listed in the catalogs of printmaking suppliers such as Graphic Chemical & Ink, New York Central Art Supply, and Renaissance Graphic Arts.

For most photopolymer work on a flatbed cylinder press, stiff, sticky, high viscosity ink will provide a crisp image with even coverage. Viscosity is a measure of internal resistance to flow. Ink should "slump" not "puddle." Too low a viscosity can cause fill-in and image gain. Viscosity drops with increasing temperature and may often require alteration during an extended print run. Modifications are accomplished with the abstemious application of the correct additive.

Some printers will mix differently formulated inks to achieve certain effects. Ink manufacturers warn this will only bring out the worst characteristics of either formulation. Different kinds of work demand different kinds of ink and it might be safer to find the right ink for the job rather than to invent concoctions that only an alchemist could appreciate. On the other hand, color work and viscosity alteration often require some combination of inks—but even here it is best to stick with compatibility among brands and formulations.

Wrap a wide strip of clear packaging tape around the labels of newly acquired cans to prevent manufacturer's identification from becoming covered with ink during subsequent use. Unidentifiable or inherited ink cans are best discarded. When removing ink from a can use the bottom edge of the ink knife (while twisting the can in a circular fashion) to take a level amount of ink from the surface. Do not dig down into the body of the ink. When you have removed the ink required for a job immediately cover the ink can. Ink must be preserved from exposure to oxygen. When work is completed clean the top edge of the can and inside cover lip with solvent. When dry apply Vaseline to these surfaces. Before closing the can place a paper skin on the surface of the ink to seal it. **Once ink has become encrusted it is difficult to save.** Pieces of crust will find their way into the working pool, adhering to rollers and transferring to printing surfaces, reproducing as hickeys (tiny blobs on printed type or images).

Other concerns are the accumulation of paper dust during an edition run and rag lint on rollers. Softer papers are inherently dustier than hard surfaced papers and cutting stacks of paper can add to the problem. If dust accumulation is noticeable it is advisable to blow it out of the press with compressed air and clean the ink

rollers. Lintless rags are necessary when cleaning forms and rollers
and careful wiping of the rollers before they are inked will prevent
lint "worms" from attaching themselves to inked surfaces of plates.

**To obtain the best possible inking and impression, use papers
specifically formulated for relief printing** such as *mouldmade*
and handmade printmaking papers (avoid externally sized papers
made for watercolor use). These papers are particularly receptive
to ink and impression when printed damp. They work up quickly
to edition state and loss rates are greatly reduced. There are also
a number of text weight mouldmades that perform well without
dampening. These include papers from Hahnemühle (such as Bugra
Butten) and Zerkall (particularly the Frankfurt line). Machine made
papers formulated for offset or planographic printing, while much
less expensive than printmaking papers, are not often the most suitable for letterpress printing. Certain "cushionable" papers, however,
such as Crane's Lettra (a paper originally formulated for engraving,
and recently revived) have become quite popular with contemporary letterpress printers for deep impression printing.

18. Impression

If both flatbase and photopolymer plate are precise and true to the technical requirements of the press, very little difficulty will be encountered with either impression or inking. Photopolymer plates are very forgiving and makeready and inking problems are considerably lessened with their use. *Impression* tends to read fairly evenly with photopolymer plates because they are resilient. Problems with impression or inking are easily resolved with minimal makeready, *underlays*, or roller support adjustments. Papers not normally printed easily with metal type, such as handmades with foreign materials embedded in them, can often be printed with photopolymer plates without fear of damage to the printing surface or, to a lesser degree, oddities in impression.

There has been some concern expressed about image rendering problems when printing with "deep impression." These include distortion of the printing surface and loss of detail, particularly isolated lines and dots, where the relief structure is inherently less supportive. This will vary in incidence dependent upon the type of plate and/or the base. To some extent these problems are more commonplace with thick plates than thin plates as the photopolymer structure is less supportive, and more likely the case with polyester-backed plates than steel-backed. Distortion can also be attributed to compression because of weakness or inconsistency in plate or adhesive or base structure. Magnetic rubber sheeting, for instance, will give under pressure and impression is transferred not only to the substrate, but to the steel backing of the plate as well. The indentation to the thin steel can actually increase during an edition run causing less and less impression to be transferred to the paper.

There are a number of opinions on the correct degree of impression to be applied to paper. Contemporary letterpress printers invariably find that their graphic designer clients expect a vividly visual impression, the basic essence of letterpress. There is disagreement whether deep impression is a desirable goal, but this is usually an aesthetic consideration made without regard for quality presswork. **Impression is historically a technical concern; it is correct when it facilitates consistently even inking.** Fine printers sought to reproduce the letterforms or image with a clean, crisp look, with just enough ink to cover the surface completely but not so much as to cause ink spread. This was primarily achieved through careful adjustment of ink film and impression.

To achieve even impression when printing with multiple bases, they must be balanced to the bed. This can often be done with slips of .0005" or .001" underlay material. Be very cautious not to drag particulate matter under the base(s) or to use underlay material with kinks or tears, as these can fold over and give unwanted increased impression. An even impression across the form is determined by printing a heavyweight proof sheet without inking. Examine the sheet in cross light to detect variance in impression from one edge to another.

If impression is off from one side of the bed to another and cannot be corrected by turning the bases end for end, in one configuration or another, the most likely problem is that cylinder carriage bearings are off and need to be adjusted. This would, of course, hold true for balancing a single base as well. Impression balance has always been a common practice on iron platen presses, but it has been relatively ignored on the cylinder press. Bearing adjustments have become a more significant element in providing optimal press performance as the result of the growing use of photopolymer plates— cylinder misalignment was not as easily detected with a metal type form. Cylinder carriage bearing adjustments are best left to a press mechanic. It is highly recommended that this be done on a periodic basis. As a press ages, its moving parts wear, and they need to be readjusted or replaced.

To some extent there is just so much that can be done. The beds of cylinder proof presses were not parallelized in the first place: Vandercook's manufacturing tolerances, for instance, allowed for a variance of .002" across the face of the bed. As such, **balancing the printing surface to the press is more often a juggling act than a science.**

Part IV:
Working With Digital Type

Examples of font modification

Printing digital type
Printing digital type

Stone Print at 40-point. Second instance is adjusted for titling or as configured for letterpress printing. At text sizes, only the slightest reduction
in character stroke weight is necessary – much further adjustment would
likely result in letterform breakup. It is important that font metrics (math-
ematical coding for hinting, kerning pairs, and the like) be retained (as revealed here in the identical settings). Carefully tended, the relief process
will yield a letterform similar in weight to the original. Note: Since Post-
Script Type 1 fonts do not share kerning pairs (one to another), compositional adjustments that integrate differing fonts (character transpositions,
size-ranking, etc.) require attentive manual kerning.

R R R R R

Stone Print at 120/40-point. First instance is unaltered. Second instance is
as adjusted in previous example. The thinning effect does not alter the outside parameters of the character. Third instance reveals the consequence of
too much adjustment; note the letterform breakup at the lower juncture
of bowl and stem. Close inspection reveals its beginning in the second instance, but this might not otherwise be detected, and diminishes with size
reduction. This turns into a slight (and acceptable) fillet in the size-reduced
third instance. Further reduction of primary stem weights (without altering thinner strokes and serifs) is possible, but this requires a sophisticated
knowledge of font-editing procedures. In this regard, the aberration could
be eliminated with a slight adjustment of the character's outline path.

*This specimen of modified and unmodified Stone Print type by the author
is reproduced from an early edition of this book.*

19. Digital Type

Since the standardization of font formats nearly two decades ago, digital type foundries have amassed huge libraries of typeface designs. A number of foundries began to revive historically significant faces as well as develop original, classically inspired designs. Several of the libraries of previous type technologies are represented by digital foundries who were, in many instances, themselves survivors from earlier periods: Berthold, Enschedé Font Foundry, Lanston Type (held by P22), Letraset, Monotype Imaging (holder of Agfa, Compugraphic, ITC, Linotype, Monotype Typography), Neufville Digital (holder of designs from various European metal type foundries), PhotoLettering (held by House Industries). Various foundries revived typefaces from defunct companies such as ATF and Ludlow. Other foundries were new with the digital era but shared similar concerns: Adobe Systems, Bitstream, Carter & Cone Type, Dutch Type Library, Font Bureau, Hoefler & Frere-Jones, LetterPerfect, P22, Porchez Typofonderie, Stone Type Foundry, Storm Type Foundry. In recent years most new font development is directed toward web applications but a significant body of typefaces for print usage exists today, far more than at any other time in history.

Although there are a great many digital fonts available, it is best to err on the side of caution in selection; a useful strategy is to acquire only fonts of aesthetic *and* technical merit from established foundries. Several early-twentieth-century historic private presses abstemiously produced work with only a few typefaces. Though this goes against the grain of contemporary practice it is well worth keeping in mind. **Like everything else in life, buy the best you can afford.** Lewis Allen's statement on the selection of metal type, "choose only after thorough study, for inferior tools corrode the spirit," is as appropriate today as it was in 1969, when he published *Printing with the Handpress*. High quality digital type is easily the equal, both technically and aesthetically, of any foundry type made in the twentieth century.

20. Configuring Digital Type for Letterpress

Unfortunately, there are problems to be dealt with when digital typefaces are printed letterpress. Typefaces designed for the digital environment, which has an inordinate amount of technical demands, are not necessarily going to translate well on the letterpress page. Contemporary design practices rarely take into account the unique requirements of letterpress relief technology. Letterpress printing is unique in that it has ink spread, or *density gain*, which accumulates and causes a thickening and distortion of letterform outline with impression.

It has been said that allowances were made for ink spread in the design and production of pre-twentieth-century metal typefaces, though this may not actually have been the case. More likely, due to craft rivalries, the punchcutter would not have denigrated his craft and technique for the inadequacies of the printer. In Manuel typographique (1764), Pierre Simon Fournier emphasized, "It is not right to blame the letter for the fault of the ink." Ink spread is more an explanatory term for printed character distortion that appeared with the turn-of-the-century photographic revival of historical typefaces (redrawn and engraved on pattern matrices with the newly developed pantograph punch-cutting machine). The anomaly, as captured by the camera, was revealed as a problem of some concern. **Historically, as per Joseph Moxon, inadequately printed characters were either "fat" or "lean" and further commentary was not necessary.**

Also, the physical employment of type, whether metal or digital, in letterpress printing, has changed over time. Most traditional typefaces were designed in an era of lighter or surface impression where the highest standard was to "kiss the page." Many contemporary printers (and their customers) prefer a heavy impression and "punch it deep." This can sometimes cause issues, particularly with type from earlier times.

Similar to metal typefaces, digital typefaces do thicken when printed letterpress; but worse, and uniquely, not all characters may thicken with the same consistency. This is because design allowances *are not made* for probable outline distortion caused by poor presswork and over-inking. Whether using photopolymer plates or metal type, increased impression and ink accumulation will cause letterform thickness to appreciate. Digital type designers Hrant Papazian and the late Justin Howes have both, independently, calculated that letterpress ink gain amounts to a minimum increase of 5%. Add to that industry technical reports that suggest another probable 5% due to "exposure gain" during the processing of film negatives—a possible image gain of 10% beyond what the negative reveals.

Another significant defect of most digital typefaces is that they also lack the optical sizing characteristics often accounted for in metal type. Many metal designs were subtly altered throughout their size range to compensate for optical anomalies—an approach based on the method of the punchcutter who intuitively redesigned the various sizes as a matter of course. The invention of the pantograph, however, allowed metal type manufacturers to group relative type sizes in ranges (optical scaling) and this became common practice. Digital typefaces are generally designed as a single master at small text size—usually between 8- to 12-point, an unfortunate convention inherited from the photofilm composition years. All other sizes are extrapolations of this core size. Thus, 72-point would actually be 10-point expanded 720%. Consequently, at that extrapolation, letterforms are optically distorted; the weight of strokes and serifs appears heavy, curves are thickened, counters appear overly large, and letterform spacing is inconsistent with letterform structure.

Technical developments such as Adobe's multiple-axis fonts— especially those equipped with an optical scale axis—are attempts to address this problem. These fonts include programming for automatically creating interpolated versions of the character set. Their weight or width or optical scale can be increased or decreased between existing instances of the letterforms. For the book arts review, *Bookways*, the printer Bradley Hutchinson configured Adobe Minion MM for relief printing by expanding the character width, compensating for the reduction in weight.

There are also a number of digital typefaces from foundries such as Adobe, Monotype Imaging, Carter & Cone, and Hoefler & Frere-Jones that are **designed at larger sizes for corresponding output.** Because of this they often perform well when printed letterpress. These large-sized faces are best used at not less than about 18-point, however, as the opposite problem arises. Weight of strokes and serifs attenuate, counters fill, and character fit appears crowded.

Another approach initiated by ITC was the tried and true redrawing of typefaces in a range of sizes, i.e., optical scaling. Initially conceived as a multiple-axis font, ITC Bodoni was released as separate fonts in 6-, 12-, and 72-point—each representing a redesign of the character set per size. ITC Founder's Caslon was similarly released in 12-, 30-, and 42-point (as well as 8-line). **Subsequently, the typeface's designer, Justin Howes, carried the idea to its logical, historical conclusion by extending the font set with *true optical sizing***—and offering it through his foundry H W Caslon & Co in 8-, 10-, 12-, 14-, 18-, 22-, 24-, 30-, 36-, 42-, 48-, 60-, and 72-point (and the 8-line). Adobe, which discontinued its multiple-axis line when it abandoned the PostScript Type 1 font format, offers *size-optimized fonts*, known as Opticals, in the OpenType font format.

The Rialto font from the Austrian foundry dfTYPE is not only size-optimized, its Pressa variant is actually designed for letterpress printing and field tested on a flatbed cylinder proof press during its production. The italic in particular reveals alterations such as modified serif lengths, sharpened junctures, and ink trapping.

The vast majority of digital fonts, however, require slight alteration to configure them for letterpress. A letterform's main strokes (arm, leg, lobe, stem, tail) require subtle reduction in weight without significantly affecting minor strokes (fillets, junctures, serifs). This is accomplished with font-editing software, e.g., FontLab Studio or Fontographer, but extreme caution and attention to procedure are required when using software that can modify existing fonts. Altering a font can remove font metrics (technical information that ensures proper spacing, kerning, alignment, and the like). It is prudent to thoroughly test altered fonts before use. *[See chapters 23 and 24 for examples of font modification sequences.]*

Ultimately, the characters comprising the text block need a uniform color and harmony. The goal is to reduce the overall density of the letterforms without altering their individual integrity. Some characters, mostly those with severe vertical forms, I, l, 1, might require further attention. Typographic adjustments made during composition (not normally feasible for the compositor of handset type) may also be required—minute reduction in the size of capital letters or punctuation sets (size-ranking), slight modification of character-set width, delicate letterspacing of small *point size* settings, etc. **Niceties such as these are the hallmark of fine composition in any era.** The Southern California printer Saul Marks, of the Plantin Press, made similar adjustments (subtle typeface and character transpositions, point size reductions, and the like) to his Monotype *matrix cases*—and his machine composition was as sublime as it gets.

There are some digital typefaces that convert well to letterpress simply through anomalies in their production. The most notable example of this was Lanston Type's digitization of a portion of Lanston Monotype Company's historic type library from the original brass master patterns. The masters were pulled as reverse proofs on a Vandercook proof press, then scanned and digitized, with the result that at text sizes the digital recreations are exacting replications of the metal type designs. Lanston's Caslon Oldstyle, No. 337 prints well from photopolymer plates with no modifications whatsoever and quite nicely captures the nuances of the original.

Other fonts that seem almost too light and spindly for adequate digital work, such as several of Monotype Imaging's revived machine composition faces or historical renditions like Hoëfler & Frere-Jones's Requiem and Didot, perform well for letterpress without alteration.

21. Pre-Press Cautions and Considerations

There are particularities with photopolymer plates that differ from photomechanical engravings or metal type and are thus to be considered in regard to presswork. During exposure the subsurface relief of a photopolymer plate grows upward and fills in during photopolymerization; the longer the exposure the shallower the final relief structure. This property of photopolymer is why it can render small details—such as hairline rules, isolated dots, type, and halftones—so accurately. This subsurface relief growth ensures a stable structure to the printing surface. Since this growth is accelerated in regard to surface area proximity it can, however, be a concern and exposure rates should be modified to take this into account, especially if presswork cannot effectively resolve problems caused by the shallow *drainage pattern.*

The surface tack of photopolymer greatly contributes to its print-ability, but relief areas share this characteristic and tackiness can aggravate accumulation of ink and paper dust in the shallower areas. It is therefore crucial that plates are kept clean during an edition run as such debris can transfer a blurring effect to the printed image. This is particularly a problem with halftones and their very shallow relief. Always clean the plate with a fast drying type or plate wash using a tight weave, lintless cloth and blow out with a spray of compressed air. In cases of relief contamination use a soft dental brush (for gums) or a horsehair plate brush to gently irrigate the affected area.

A concern in this regard is bridging, where print areas in relative proximity share a shallow relief, and accumulated ink can form a visible printed bridge between them. This is sometimes the case with digital letterforms where character settings may be a bit too close. Correct this phenomenon at the prepress stage, before you finalize your typography, by carefully examining your proofing and make adjustments through modification of kerning pairs, either with font-editing software or by kerning or tracking within the page layout program. Similar precautions should be undertaken, whenever possible, with illustrative matter.

Another concern is the relationship of *aperture* to thickness of plate. A small aperture does not permit significant ultraviolet light travel throughout the plate during exposure; consequently, an adequate support structure may not form at the plate's floor. Thus, isolated dots and fine lines may not hold up during presswork with thick plates, especially if impression is severe. The real solution to this is the realization of this possible problem and preparation for it at the prepress stage by slightly increasing the relative weight of the imaging.

Since the standard relative reverse relief depth for letterpress plates is .30 mm (with slight variance between brands) no matter what their thickness, there is no advantage in using thicker plates for the purpose of a deeper than normal impression. While photopolymer plates are certainly capable of debossing and even embossing, it is not their forte as the shallower relief—especially in letterform counters and closely rendered details—is not visually appropriate in relationship to the depth of the impression well, and can result in paper surface bulging and even breakage, as well as ink fill-in.

Halftones are a particular problem with letterpress as they are, technically, planar surfaces, and have no affinity with the relief process. They can be printed with some success if certain practices are followed. They print best on hard, thin, smooth surfaced papers with minimal impression, and need a hard, tight packing, and minimum roller pressure and ink film laydown. If the edging of a halftone begins to darken during presswork the plate should be carefully cleaned to halt further fill-in. Re-check rollers at this time to ensure they are at the correct setting.

Prepress preparation generally requires no less than 20% gray (or surface drop out may occur) and no more than 87% gray (or surface solidification may occur) with all contrast built into the mid-grays. This will vary dependent upon final film negative resolution and lpi. Since letterpress printed halftones often appear washed out and lackluster, it can often be useful to print a duplicate B/W of the image beneath the halftone, as a form of duotone, to provide sharpness to specific details and overall contrast emphasis to the image. Configured appropriately, with judicious use of color, this can often add a bit of flair to the image, though it may take some experimentation, and exacting registration, to get it right.

In this regard, since registration is quite difficult with photopolymer plates, **any color work that requires several passes and exacting registration might easier be accomplished through the use of multiple bases** to which each plate is registered separately.

22. Digital Type Foundries Respond to Letterpress

Previously published as, "An Affinity by Design: Digital Type Foundries Respond to Letterpress" in *Parenthesis: The Journal of the Fine Press Book Association*, Number 7, November 2002. Reprinted here with minor editorial corrections.

For well over the past decade fine press printers have increasingly turned to the photopolymer plate process as the alternative source for metal type. In recent years the productive use of metal type in the overall studio-letterpress community has declined, but to a great extent this is no longer due just to dwindling resources. While not all would agree, the advantages and capabilities of the computer in rendering traditional typography, along with the high printability of photopolymer plates, have proved the process beyond dispute. Residual resistance to the digital/photopolymer process is now less and less based on its technical capabilities, but more on the technique itself. It violates the romanticized view of historical letterpress. This is its cardinal sin, for which there is little forgiveness.

What plagues the photopolymer process is not these considerations, but the nature of digital type itself. It is not that digital type is inferior to metal type, either technically or aesthetically, but that it is simply not designed for the relief process. (Many metal typefaces, it should be noted, do not perform well when printed letterpress either. This is self-evident to any seasoned printer, but is rarely acknowledged.)

The printer of photopolymer plates, however, does stand at a unique disadvantage to the printer of metal type. The physical formation of the photopolymer plate letterforms, though facilitated by the technical processes that are available to the printer, have not been undertaken at a previous stage in the technology. Metal type is cast at the foundry or on the printer's casting machine and is immutable, though the quality of the casting may vary. The printer works with the physical form of the typeface he or she has been given. The processing of photopolymer plates is much more fraught with the possibilities of disruption at any intermediary step. Even if these steps are taken care of exactingly, the printer is still dependent upon the very first step in the process: the proper configuration of a digital typeface. **Digital typefaces face two age-old problems for which they are not equipped: ink spread and lack of** optical size compensation.

These problems also affect metal typefaces. With the invention of the pantograph-engraving machine in the late nineteenth century, for instance, twentieth-century typefaces themselves had significantly reduced optical size ranges. Typeface designs were scaled to fit a range of group sizes. Ink spread, a thickening effect of the letterform that is unique to relief printing, is caused by impression and accumulating ink gain. This has always been a persistent demon to be controlled by the concerned printer, but the term itself came into currency more as a consequence of twentieth-century revivals of historic typefaces. Typeface designers have traditionally viewed it as an obscuring effect, rather than a problem to be dealt with technically. The punchcutter's view was perhaps the same. In his *Manuel typographique* (1764), the great typefounder Pierre Simon Fournier declared, "It is not right to blame the letter for the fault of the ink."

The digital environment is quite complex, and a technically sound typeface must perform well under a variety of diverse conditions: viewing devices ranging from the smartphone to the large screen, printing devices ranging from low resolution dot matrix to high resolution imagesetter. It has to work with varied forms of print delivery systems, such as inkjet, laser, film-based. It has to function on screen, as print, in electronic transmission. It must set well in the lowliest of text-based programs as well as perform the typographic requirements demanded by sophisticated page-layout programs. Not all digital typefaces function in all these aspects, but to some extent professional design practices ensure such capability in the more sophisticated releases.

The evolutionary process of digital type has not been as rapid as one might assume. A good part of the latter third of the twentieth century went into its development, and at every step of the way it had to satisfy parallel developments in electronic technology. At no point in this evolution was any serious consideration given to the unique restraints of the letterpress process, nor should it have been expected.

Digital typefaces also inherited the dubious typographic conventions of the preceding printing technology, that of *photomechanical typesetting.* With a notable exception or two, photofilm did away with optical size ranging entirely. In following this practice, digital faces are traditionally offered in only one point size, usually 9- or 10-point. All other representations are then extrapolations of this core size. Thus 72-point could actually be 10-point scaled to 720 percent. For a typographer this is problematic in that there is little harmony in weight between the sizes; as a face increases in size it just gets thicker and appears bulky and there is no built-in compensation for this. For legibility, smaller sizes need a large x-height, increased weight and width, opened counters, and wider settings. Larger sized faces need a reduction in weight and width, with serifs refined to a visually pleasing thinness.

Hand punchcutters from the mid-fifteenth to the late nineteenth century are thought to have redesigned a typeface as a matter of course, on a per size basis, building in a natural optical compensation as they graved and filed the letterforms on the ends of the steel punches. Though the pantograph-engraving machine allowed this practice to wither away, **there was still an attempt throughout the first half of the twentieth century to build in certain optical size ranges in metal type designs.** With notable exception, firms selling machine composition matrices commonly restricted their ranges. Monotype often provided only a small text range (6- to 10-point), a text range (12- to 14-point), an intermediary range, and a large size range. Some firms, such as Linotype, had more diverse ranges, but not by much. With the introduction of photofilm there seemed no point in continuing the practice as typesetters could just scale sizes photographically, and were not willing to pay for ranging. Why buy four versions of one typeface when you could buy four typefaces? Without client resistance there was no need to modify the practice.

The development of digital type followed the same path but, oddly enough, took more seriously the gift the past had handed over to it. The first digital typefoundry, Bitstream Inc., was co-founded by the well-seasoned type designer Matthew Carter, who as a young man cut punches at the Enschedé foundry. When Adobe Systems Inc. began to manufacture digital typefaces, they brought onboard individuals who had serious interest in letterforms: professional calligraphers, several with ties to the fine press community. Adobe began to offer original designs that had a historical connection to metal type and they patterned the best offerings of our typographic history, including character forms that were rarely seen in the photofilm years: small capitals, oldstyle figures, alternate characters, and ornaments. Most exciting of all, they revived the type specimen book. Adobe had a strong influence on the industry, as it had also developed one of the more sophisticated font formats, PostScript Type 1.

A significant development at Adobe was its eventual line of multiple master typefaces, the first of which was released in 1991. These were unique in offering optical size ranging. A multiple master face came equipped with one or more axes. These axes were primary re-drawings of variance, which Adobe called a dynamic range. A weight axis would carry a lighter version of a design as well as a heavier version. Adobe also provided instances of re-drawings at selected intervals between the primaries. Thus a multiple master weight axis might carry a number of weight variations built into the face. Multiple master fonts included a software program that allowed users the possibility of *interpolating* between instances to create their own instance. Adobe eventually offered faces with a variety of design axes: weight, width, style (used primarily in applications equipped for font substitution) and, significantly, optical size.

In 1992, the influential book arts review *Bookways* made the switch from machine composition to photopolymer plates. First, its printer, Bradley Hutchinson, without announcing the shift, made the transition in issue #3 from the metal face, Monotype Bembo, that had been used in the first two issues of the journal, to polymer plates set from Monotype's digital Bembo (with ascenders & descenders adjusted slightly in Fontographer). Subscribers were apparently unaware of the transition until issue #5, when *Bookways* printed a side-by-side comparison of the hot metal Bembo and the modified polymer version. With issue #6, *Bookways* shifted to Adobe's Minion, and later moved to the multiple master version of Minion. The MM version was modified for letterpress printing by reducing the stroke of the face on its weight axis, increasing the optical size axis to open the counters, and slightly expanding the letterform width. *Bookways* issue #10 explains this evolution. *[Editor's note: this paragraph has been modified from the original publication to reflect new information from Bradley Hutchinson.]*

Interestingly, in 1994, when Adobe released its version of the historic Jenson as a multiple master (Adobe Jenson MM), it included in its remarkable specimen book a tipped-in letterpress printed poem with a caption reading:

> The use of polymer plates to print digital type by letterpress has become popular in recent years. This method combines the convenience and flexibility of typesetting on a computer with the traditional look of letterpress printing. With multiple master fonts that include axes for optical size and weight, a custom instance can be generated to better suit this method of printing. In letterpress, ink spread occurs naturally, resulting in a denser printed image. To compensate for this in the printed poem, a finer and lighter multiple master font was used.

Unfortunately, with its co-development of the OpenType font format, Adobe abandoned further offerings in its PostScript Type 1 line. Though several of the multiple master fonts have been reformatted they are now only equipped with "opticals," the existent multiple master primaries and pre-configured instances.

Generally, digital typefaces need to be altered in a font-editing program such as Fontographer or FontLab to make them more suitable for letterpress printing. This is a fairly simple task but must be approached quite carefully as altered faces may not function properly if not configured correctly. But this is only an alternate solution as, unless one is quite familiar with such programs, only a slight weight reduction is possible without changing the characteristics of the letterforms or damaging the font metrics.

Not all digital typefaces need to be configured for letterpress. A number of them work quite well without any alteration whatsoever. These tend to be from foundries with some historical

connection such as Monotype Typography Ltd. or Linotype AG
that had inherited large typeface libraries from the years when
their predecessors sold matrices for machine composition. One
of the last faces released by Monotype Typography, before it
merged with Agfa, was Monotype Pastonchi, a quite near replication of the machine composition face issued by The Monotype
Corporation Ltd. Unaltered digital revivals of historical typefaces,
however, are the exception rather than the rule. Some faces
such as HTF Didot Light, issued by The Hoefler Type Foundry
Inc., function quite well for letterpress in that they are almost
too spindly and anemic for general digital work. Other than
Adobe, however, the only digital foundry previously "friendly" to
letterpress was Lanston Type Co. Ltd., which issued a number of
digital faces reproduced from the American Lanston Monotype
Machine Company's historic type library. Lanston Type acquired
the remnants of Lanston Monotype, along with the original brass
master patterns in 1989.

Lanston Type's goal was to digitize the faces with all the unique
spatial and visual characteristics of the original typeface so that
the eventual type, when printed, would look as if produced on a
Monotype casting machine. All the variant characters associated
with the original font scheme would be made, including small
caps, ligatures, ranging and non-ranging figures, tied, swash,
and accented characters, alternate short or long descenders, etc.
At the time, this was quite an ambitious undertaking; no other
digital foundry was offering such amenities. (These were not, by
the way, often available to the printer in the metal type era, as
alternate character matrices were optional purchases, and very
few composition houses carried them.) The large masters were
pulled as reverse proofs on a Vandercook proof press, then
scanned and digitized, with the result that at text sizes the digital

recreations were exacting replications of the metal type designs. These digital reenactments perform remarkably well when printed letterpress. Lanston Type digitized a good portion of the Lanston Monotype library but the project came to a sudden halt in the early 1990s. There is, however, recent intention to revive the endeavor.

Digital faces such as these do to some extent address the problem of letterform weight exacerbated by ink spread, but unlike Adobe's multiple masters, there is still no compensation for optical size range. Optical size range can be built into a digital typeface by creating several alternate weight instances with a font-editing program (as mentioned above). But this is not as desirable as if optical size range was offered directly from the typeface designer. Several digital foundries, such as Adobe, Agfa Monotype, Carter & Cone Type Inc., and Hoefler Type Foundry have released certain typefaces drawn at larger size with the rec-ommendation that they not be used at text sizes. If used properly, these can provide satisfactory results when printed letterpress.

An interesting development occurred as an offspring of multiple master technology and possibly of these other considerations. In 1994, International Typeface Corporation completed work on a historically accurate typeface based on the types of Giambattista Bodoni, which was unique in that it was a digital typeface issued in the optical size ranging pattern common to twentieth-cen-tury machine composition practice. Originally intended as a multiple master typeface, ITC Bodoni was brought out instead in three separate fonts: 6-, 12-, and 72-point, each representing a redesign of the character set. (This is now the pattern for Adobe OpenType fonts released with opticals.) This was followed in 1998, by ITC Founder's Caslon (based on specimens and printed text sheets of types by 18th century type designer William Caslon), which was released in 12-, 30-, and 42-point, as well as an 8-line based on wood type. These were less redesigns than exacting replications of originals by type historian and designer Justin Howes.

Revivals have been a part of digital type releases almost right from the beginning, but the idea of resurrecting historic typefaces first appears about mid-nineteenth century with the original Caslon revival by the foundries of that era. It does not begin across the board until the late nineteenth century—under the popular sway of William Morris and his Kelmscott Press, and also as a consequence of increased consumer access to the photographic process. This was a two-phase revival that reached its typographic fruition in the 1920s (primarily conducted by the Monotype companies, British and American). One of the more interesting faces produced by Monotype at that time was Poliphilus (1922), which was based on Aldine types but refreshingly, rather than being completely redesigned, was left somewhat with its original "printed" look.

Only relatively recently have digital type designers thought to go beyond this and preserve historic faces in situ. Besides Justin Howes' work, Hoefler Type Foundry's Historical Allsorts (a remarkable specimen collection comprised of the Fell Types—Roman, Small Caps, Italics; St. Augustin Civilité—with alternates; English Textura—with alternates; and Great Primer Uncials), which was released in 1997, is an attempt at rendering historic faces without any designer interpretation or intrusion. Characters from original texts were traced algorithmically by software and left be. Hoefler's comment on the faces, that they "have a pleasantly arrhythmic pace... and overall, an agreeably (if not ironically) un-digital warmth," hits the mark. Unlike the ITC revivals, however, the faces that comprise this unique experiment are not size optimized.

Astonishingly, in 2001, Justin Howes reissued Founder's Caslon from his newly "claimed" foundry, H. W. Caslon and Company Limited, in 8-, 10-, 12-, 14-, 18-, 22-, 24-, 30-, 36-, 42-, 48-, 60-, and 72-point, as well as in 8-line. Each size offered is based on a specimen showing at that size. In doing so, the twenty-first century was given a gift from the past that the twentieth may never have had—a fully size-ranged type design with true optical compensation.

The reissue consists of some 68 fonts in the fourteen sizes: Caslon Text consisting of 8- to 18-point and Caslon Display, consisting of 22- to 72-point (also included with the Display is the 8-line Poster and a suite of Caslon Ornaments). Separately available is a beta version of the fonts in the OpenType format as well as Founder's Caslon 1776, a singular font based on the text type (at 14-point) used by the Philadelphia printer John Dunlap for the printing of the Declaration of Independence.

Founder's Caslon is an "exact and scholarly resuscitation." Howes' digital reconstruction attempts to bring back "a simple, really basic typographic tool which earlier designers had been able to take for granted from about 1720 up to about 1980." By reproducing from high-resolution scans of new proofs of existent founder's type (or where not available, from printed text and specimen sheets), he was able to "sidestep the conceptual problems associated with re-interpreting punch-cut letters in terms of pencil outlines and computer curve points." He suggests his Caslon is "richer in texture than designs based on a single master design, and still with something of the vagaries and beauties inherent in punchcutting and letterpress printing."

Indeed, Howes felt no need to attend to the problem of ink spread in his digitization:

> The irregularities of letterpress printing are also faithfully captured by the process. I see no reason to remove them, since they become troublesome only under high magnification and, at normal size, make an important but virtually invisible contribution to the text of the page... Ligature Caslon [Founder's Caslon], if it cannot produce diversity, makes an attempt to reproduce it.

Howes' work on Founder's Caslon is quite serious. His scholarly analyses of "Caslon's Punches and Matrices" (which includes a detailed inventory of the existing Caslon materials) was published in *Matrix*, in 2000. He had access to the type, punch, and matrix collections of St Bride Printing Library, as well as the Type Museum of Stephenson Blake and Company Limited (Stephenson Blake acquired the remnants of the Caslon firm when it went into liquidation in 1936).

Measured by contemporary standards, the original Caslon old face form is quite quirky in its spacing and lining attributes—the letterspacing is unusually wide and the alignment of the individual characters is not "regularized." The letterforms themselves suffer from odd contrasts in stroke and color. The face seems designed less for the harmony and details of its letterforms than for the intriguing pattern of its text setting, which provides to it a remarkably deceptive, simple and fluent legibility.

William Caslon cut, in 1722, the first roman for the typeface that is now the ancestor to most faces by that name. It was derived from Dutch type, which then dominated the English market. The popularity of the typeface in years to follow, however, gave England an international reputation as the leader in the type industry. The Caslon old face fell out of use by the turn of the 18th century (the Caslon specimen book of 1805 shows no such fonts) but was revived in 1844 when the Chiswick Press began using it in its books.

In America, the old face style had degraded over the years by successive recuttings. Following the English resurrection, the first "authentic" American version of Caslon dates from 1859, when the Laurence J. Johnson foundry began issuing an old face derived from "borrowed Caslon foundry punches." By 1892, the American Caslon revival was in full swing. Interestingly, most twentieth-century American Caslon revivals were based on the Johnson types. In the digital era there have been several important revivals, notably Lanston Type's replication of Lanston Monotype Caslon Oldstyle 337 (considered the closest rendition of the Johnson Caslon), Adobe Caslon (based on Caslon foundry specimen sheets from 1738 and 1786), and Matthew Carter's Big Caslon, based on titling sizes that appeared in Caslon's famous broadsheet specimen of 1734.

Most Caslon revivals, however, even these digital versions, are not historically truthful to the originals as they are regularized versions; old face style letterforms were, and are, considered too eccentric for contemporary taste. Founder's Caslon, on the other hand, has an engaging authenticity about it that hasn't been seen since the decline of commercial punchcutting. To ensure this, Howes deliberately eliminated inauthentic characters added to the various Caslons since the revival began. To preserve the integrity of Founder's Caslon he has similarly removed from his definitive version the oldstyle italic figures that are proffered with ITC Founder's Caslon, and only included those swash and alternate forms that were created by William Caslon himself. The reissued Founder's Caslon also carries

with it character forms that are not in the ITC version, such as
a full long-s ligature set. Also included are original Caslon tied
characters, small caps, oldstyle nut-fractions, and so forth. Even
the 8-line poster font is based on the only authentic wood letter
version of Caslon old face (issued in the 1890s).

Working with Founder's Caslon is a refreshing experience and
not too dissimilar from that of standing at the composing bank.
The compositor needs to select the font of that size rather than
sizing. This might be a bit awkward at first for those who have
never handset metal type. And even the most tempered of typographers might be reluctant to adjust the kerning of oddly spaced
characters (Howes, in fact, did not initially intend to apply
kerning to the fonts). Since the face literally changes in its design
per size it can be a bit perplexing and one might be tempted to
violate the intention of the typeface by using one designed size
at other sizes. One anomaly, an unusual jump in size from the
10-point (Long-Primer) to the 12-point (Pica) is not atypical in
a metal type design, but could force the compositor to either
shrink the Pica or enlarge the Long-Primer. Howes has acknowledged the usefulness of the further addition of an 11-point (Small
Pica). This would serve better in the digital Caslon than it might
have in metal.

In his *Mechanick Exercises on the Whole Art of Printing* (1683-4),
Joseph Moxon revealed why the Small Pica could prove problematic in the printshop:

> I account it no great discretion in a Master-Printer to
> provide it; because it differs so little from the Pica, that
> unless the Workmen be carefuller than they sometimes are,
> it may be mingled with the Pica, and so the Beauty of both
> Founts may be spoil'd.

The work on Founder's Caslon (Ligature Caslon), began in 1995/6. At that time Howes was intending to include eight sizes of Caslon's Old Black ranging from 8- to 36-point, a reconstruction of Caslon's Long Primer No. 1, and William Caslon II's "Proscription" letters, as well as showings of Caslon's Greek, Hebrew, music, and script types. Since these are not part of Founder's Caslon as presently configured one can only hope that they will materialize in the new future. Interestingly, in his article, "The Compleat Caslon," which was published in *Matrix*, in 1997, there are digitized specimen showings of the Old Black and that of William Caslon II.

Howes even entertained the possibility of further optimizing Founder's Caslon specifically for letterpress. I asked him why he would offer this considering the complexity of Founder's Caslon and the amount of effort that this would take—with little expectation of return. He replied, "There's the sheer pleasure of getting it right... We all know that Caslon looks best printed on handmade paper... it should be possible for Caslon to look as good as it's ever done."

Equally amazing is the empathetic yet entirely different approach in the creation of Rialto, which was released by the Austrian foundry dfTYPE in 1999. Rialto is an original digital typeface that was designed with letterpress printing in mind. Begun in 1995, Rialto is the result of a collaboration between Lui Karner, the founder (in 1990) of the fine press Die Fischbachpresse, and the calligrapher Giovanni de Faccio. dfTYPE is the type design offspring of the press.

Representative of the new breed of fine press printer, Karner is holder of a remarkable collection of handset foundry type (which includes such rarities as Cancelleresca Bastarda, Delphin,

Elisabeth Antiqua, Lectura, Peter Jessen Schrift, Romulus, Shakespeare Antiqua, Trump Mediaeval, and Walbaum Antiqua) and prints his work (both metal and "photopolymere Druckplatten") on the highly regarded European-made FAG "Cylinder-Handpresse."

A typographic tour de force, Rialto has been released in an optically sized range of four fonts: Rialto, Rialto Piccolo, Rialto Bold (all in roman, italic, and small caps), and Rialto Titling (caps only). A recent addition is Rialto Pressa, a special version of Rialto Piccolo specifically optimized for letterpress printing with photopolymer plates. The nicely produced Rialto specimen book (which is available as a promotion) reveals the concerns that went into the design of the typeface.

Beginning with the idea that the shapes of all roman and italic lowercase derive from roman capitals (which may or may not be the case) the team of Karner and De Faccio sought to create a set of capitals that shared the characteristics of both roman and italic, attempting to develop a face that would allow for a harmonious combination of the various type forms while retaining a certain character and contrast to each. Thus the capitals are shared by both the roman and italic lowercase. **Rialto is heralded by its makers as "a bridge between calligraphy and typography."** And this was certainly my initial reaction to the face. It does not quite have the calligraphic look of typefaces that are typographic renditions of handwritten letterforms; there is, instead, an enhanced typographic feel to the face because of the calligraphic approach to its design. Rialto is uncommonly beautiful. While not an Aldine, it has a familiar Aldine typographic sensibility, but with a tempered contemporary flair.

Though based on the stone-carved letterforms of Roman

inscriptions (Capitalis Monumentalis) with an inspiration from the model of well proportioned Dutch type forms, such as those popularized by the seventeenth-century typefounder Christoffel van Dijck, Rialto's capitals are "distinct from all historical types" in that they have calligraphic serifs derived from the broad pen. The movement of the pen is also reflected in the "flow of the stems into the serifs" which imparts to them "a delicate lightness and dynamism."

Karner and De Faccio provide an interesting synopsis of the historical evolution of the height and slope of capitals in defending their relatively small cap height and degree of slope. The capitals are noticeably lower than usually presented and the rationale was that this would allow them to harmonize better with the italic. This seems to be the case and certainly sets Rialto apart. Based on historical romans, a one degree slope to the right was considered by the team to be "an important requirement for optimum legibility." The calligraphic features imparted to the capitals were also given over to the lowercase roman font, which are likewise sloped. The mark of the broad pen is revealed in the sharp angles where the stroke changes direction and in the precision of the serifs (especially the baseline serifs which have a remarkably engaging dip, extended draw, and sudden lift).

Concern for legibility is also shown in the distinctive movements of the individual letterforms relative to the x-height and in the traditional small counters provided the *a* and *e* characters. The italic was allowed upright shapes without regard to slope but to ensure harmony with the capitals the slope was held to three degrees. There is also a considered empathy with the roman in the spacing of the italics, which are set a bit wider than normal and therefore show well in text mass.

Other typographic amenities provide typographic breadth to the font. Small caps are provided for the three Rialto upper- and lowercase fonts and are unique in that they are self-spacing. The oldstyle Dutch inspired figures (e.g., Jan van Krimpen's Romanée) follow the example of the capitals and serve both the roman and italic, being set at the x-height of the small caps and supplied for both text and columnar uses. A healthy palette of ligatures is provided for both the italic and roman, including both tied-characters and a full set of long-s ligatures. Rialto also contains special characters such as early Italian italic *es is us* ligatures, a double-storied italic *g*, and variants of capitals.

Most importantly, Rialto is optically ranged. dfTYPE recommends Rialto Bold for sizes smaller than 6-point, Rialto Piccolo for sizes up to 14-point, and Rialto Regular for sizes 16-point and larger. The Titling font itself reveals clearly the weight reduction, narrow shapes, and elongated serifs necessary for display.

The special letterpress configured Rialto Pressa is absolutely remarkable. At first I could not detect any significance difference between its Roman and that of Piccolo's because I was looking for stroke or stem weight reduction. In fact, Pressa has a slightly heavier appearance. In examining the italic, I noticed outline point disturbances. When the fonts were matched at 148-point size, several alterations were apparent. The face appears to have been modified for ink trapping, as well as slightly extended serifs and changes in junctions.

Rialto is a typographer's dream. Its typographic beauty is not just skin-deep, and it is pleasing to work with. The settings require little fussing and the typographic amenities are configured to each specific font. I have found the roman lowercase combinations of *ch* and *ck* a bit too tight for my pleasure, as is the unit space setting of the parentheses, and the characters comprising the tied italics are too widely set apart, but these are quite minor quibbles compared to the deficiencies of most typefaces. All this is made up for by an unbelievably disarming italic *f* with its wonderfully exaggerated descender—a defining typeface identification mark if there ever was one.

In the Rialto specimen book there is a tiny gloss next to the description of the optical ranging capability of the typeface: "Voilà—there are no more excuses!" Lewis Allen's statement on the selection of metal type, **"choose only after thorough study, for inferior tools corrode the spirit,"** is as appropriate today as it was in 1969, when he published *Printing With the Handpress*. There are no more excuses.

23. Font Modification Sequence for Fontographer

The following is a simple yet reliable sequence for altering (reducing) the weight of PostScript Type 1 (Mac) fonts for letterpress configuration using Fontographer version 5.0.x in Mac OS X (at press time the latest version of Fontographer was 5.2.3). Earlier versions of Fontographer follow the basic procedure as developed here, but certain features of the interface will have been altered.

From Fontographer's menu bar, open the original printer font (the font to be altered) and Select All from the Edit menu. Then choose Change Weight from the Element menu. The Change Weight window provides a text edit box and several option boxes that allow you to retain characters' vertical and horizontal sizing. These should be checked. The text edit box should be set to default at -5 em units. The approximate range of usefulness is -2.5 to -7.5 em units. Note that to add weight to letterforms (for creating size optimized small text glyphs) the em unit should be 2.5 to 7.5.

Once you have completed your modifications you must rename the font to distinguish it from the original font. Do this by selecting Font Info from the Element menu. The Font Info window provides a Family Name and a Style Name text edit box. Since you are only altering from the original font leave the Family Name alone. In the Design Parameters grouping select a description appropriate to your modification: Light, ExtraLight, UltraLight, Thin. Your font name will now have the selection appended to it.

To ensure that the font has not been stripped of vital technical information you must now import bitmap data from the original font. Import Bitmaps via the File/Import/Bitmaps menu sequence. Select the bitmap suitcase of the original font. Next, import Kerning and Spacing from the File/Import/Metrics menu sequence. Again select the bitmap suitcase of the original font. Next, import Ascent/Descent from the File/Import/ Metrics menu sequence. Once more select the bitmap suitcase of the original font.

Finally, select Recalc Bitmaps from the Element menu. In this window select Recalculate Glyphs: All or Recalculate Glyphs: Changed Only or Selected Only (if you have not modified all characters in the font). Select Preserve Line Spacing before you click on Recalculate. Generate your font by choosing Generate Font Files from the File menu. Examine the various text-edit boxes in this window to make sure they are appropriate. The suitcase and printer files of the font may need to be generated separately.

You will most likely have to repeat this entire sequence several times until you find the correct weight for your new font. Make these changes in small increments, proofing the font on a laser printer at a resolution of at least 600 or preferably 1200 dpi (camera-ready quality). For best results, don't alter an already modified font. Start each test afresh from the original printer font. Eventually, of course, you should test your new font by printing it letterpress from a photopolymer plate.

OpenType fonts can be modified in Fontographer (beginning with version 5.0.x) but because of the OpenType format's complexity and variables it is sometimes difficult to get consistent, reliable results. Consequently, no attempt is made here to provide a modification sequence for that purpose.

24. Font Modification Sequence for FontLab Studio

The reader is referred to the FontLab Studio manual for more sophisticated approaches to modifying fonts or to confirm procedures mentioned in this sequence, which is appropriate for altering PostScript Type 1 (Mac) fonts using FontLab Studio version 5.0.x in Mac OS X. Earlier versions of FontLab follow somewhat the basic procedure as developed here, but certain features of the interface will have been altered.

Encoding preferences for opening and generating fonts must be configured properly in FontLab Studio. Before you open the font to be modified go to FontLab Studio Preferences and click on Opening Type 1. In this window Decompose All Composite Glyphs should be unchecked, and Generate Unicode Indexes For All Glyphs checked. Next open Generating Type 1. The two boxes at the top of the list, Make PFM file and Make AFM and INF files, are checked by default. Though you may not need these files in the Mac environment, FontLab recommends that you create them. In the panel Encoding Options choose the Select Encoding Automatically option (for standard Western Roman fonts). The check boxes Automatically Sort Glyphs and Autohint Unhinted Glyphs should be enabled. The check box Use Win-Ascent and WinDescent should not be enabled. The check box Type 1 Autohinting (on the second page of this window) should be enabled. Click Apply and then Okay.

Important note: **FontLab Studio can modify and create fonts in several platforms and font formats.** If you choose to import and export from or to any of these, your encoding preferences need to be changed to conform to the various requirements of each of them. The manual is downloadable from the FontLab site in PDF format. This provides the necessary encoding information for various formats.

To modify a font, open the menu bar option File, select Open and choose the PostScript Type 1 font you intend to alter. A Font window will open, displaying the font's character set. To modify the font, select Action from the Tools menu. This will open the Actions window (this was previously known as the Transformations window). Check the Apply To Entire Font box. In the window there are a number of "transformation" actions available. Open the Effects action. Select the Bold transformation and click on it. The Effects box that opens will allow you to make the weight adjustments. There are two weight variables, Horizontal Weight and Vertical Weight. These both default to a unit value of 20. Reduce this, initially, to a maximum of -5 on the horizontal. The vertical weight should be set at 0. Note, however, that a slight decrease or increase (-2 to 2) can be useful for adjusting the thickness of serifs and vertical stress, but you will have to experiment a bit with these values. These adjustments do not affect character proportion but to ensure this the Keep Glyph's Dimensions box must be checked. The Change Weight of the Glyph button should also be checked. To complete the transformation, click the Okay button.

Once you have completed your alterations you must rename the font to distinguish it from the original font. Do this by selecting Font Info from the File menu. This opens the Basic Set of Font Names window. Do not alter the family name. Select the proper addition to the font name in the Weight scroll box. Name your font similarly in the PS Font Name option. Then click on the Build Names Records button. Click Apply and then Okay to save your name changes. You may also have to rename the Menu Name and Font Name to correspond to your changes or they may be incorrectly identified in the Font Menu of certain applications.

To generate your font, go to the Generate Font command located in the File menu. In this window the Font Format option ASCII/ UNIX Type 1 should be chosen. Click Okay. This will save the modified outline font to a folder of your designation. Then separately go to the Generate Suitcase command (also located in the File menu), select Macintosh Type 1 and click Okay.

Note: FontLab Studio allows for several different approaches to accomplish the modification of a font's character set outlines. The sequence proffered here is patterned after the above Fontographer sequence, and yields similar results for PostScript Type 1 fonts. OpenType fonts can likewise be modified in FontLab Studio, but because of the format's complexity and variables it is sometimes difficult to get consistent, reliable results. Consequently, no attempt is made here to provide a modification sequence for that purpose.

Afterword

Most problems encountered in the printing of digital type with photopolymer plates are the result of economic shortcuts, inferior tools and materials, poor work habits, and lack of knowledge or improper instruction. In this regard the process is no different than printing with metal type. Photopolymer, however, is definitely a superior relief printing surface and the work produced can, thanks to high quality digital type and sophisticated typographic software, easily match and surpass the compositional strategies of the metal era. The disciplined skills and knowledge acquired through years of standing at the composing bank are readily transferable to the digital medium. The printed page is, of course, the final arbitrator. In that regard, in the assured hands of the fine printer, the validity of the process is indisputable.

Of even greater significance, however, is that the process of printing digital type with photopolymer plates has saved the practice of studio-letterpress from dying a whimpering death and may allow it to continue in strength well into the twenty-first century. Many of us could not have envisioned this a few decades ago, nor was it a hope that could possibly be entertained.

Editor's note: In my working lifetime, I have witnessed at first a graying of working printers during the many years it was seen as a dying craft, and later a remarkable rejuvenation as more and more young people entered the field. Presses like the Vandercook which were once little more than scrap are now sought-after tools, and letterpress printing as a craft is vibrant, alive, and ever-changing. The future of this craft is a wonderful thing to contemplate, and we wish you the best as you explore it.

About the Author

Gerald Lange is the proprietor and founder (1975) of The Bieler
Press, a small printing and publishing firm specializing in studio
letterpress, typographic design, and the publication of finely
printed limited edition books and related matter. Lange was
the first recipient of the Hertzog Award for Excellence in Book
Design. He has been involved in letterpress printing with the
photopolymer process for nearly three decades and has provided
photopolymer plate processing to the contemporary studio
letterpress community since 1995. For decades he has taught
workshops and classes at institutions including the School of the
Art Institute of Chicago, Saint John's University, the University
of Minnesota, the University of Southern California, Art Center
College of Design, the California Institute of the Arts, and Otis
College of Art and Design among others. He has lectured widely,
and taught private workshops. Lange first released *Printing
digital type on the hand-operated flatbed cylinder press* in 1998. In
2001, he founded the online site PPLetterpress to provide an
online community forum on studio-letterpress and letterpress-
related typography.

References & Suggested Reading

Lewis Allen. *Printing with the Handpress.* Allen Press, Kentfield, 1969.

[Jonathan Hoefler and various]. *Catalogue of Typefaces: Fourth Edition.* The Hoefler Type Foundry, NY. 2000.

Justin Howes. "The Compleat Caslon." *Matrix: A Review for Printers & Bibliophiles,* Herefordshire, UK. Issue number 17, 1997.

Lui Karner and Waltraud Stefan. *Rialto df: a bridge between [calligraphy and typography].* dfTYPE, Texing, Österreich. 2000.

Gerald Lange. "Intelligent Letterform Scaling: Adobe System's Forthcoming Multiple Master Font Adobe Jenson." *Bookways: A Quarterly For the Book Arts,* Austin. Number 10, January, 1994.

Gerald Lange. "Monotype Type Revivals (Part III): Lanston Type's Caslon Oldstyle 337." *The Typographer* (Typographers International Association), Washington, DC. Volume 19, Number 5, July/August, 1993.

Gerald Lange. *Printing digital type on the hand-operated flatbed cylinder press.* Bieler Press Monographs, Marina del Rey. Second Edition, 2001.

Paul Moxon. *Vandercook Presses.* Fameorshame Press, Mobile, 2015.

Robert Slimbach [and various]. *Adobe Jenson: A Contemporary Revival: A new multiple master typeface family based on the original types of Nicolas Jenson and Ludovico degli Arrighi.* Adobe Systems Incorporated, Palo Alto. 1994.

Glossary

Editor's note: We have supplied this glossary for your ease of use. If there are any terms we have not defined which you would have found helpful, or if there are any definitions which could be more accurate or clear, please send a note to info@chatwinbooks.com, *and we will address them in future printings.*

Agitator: For photopolymer platemakers, the agitator is that piece, usually a bristly, brush-like surface, against which the exposed plate is rubbed to remove the unhardened polymer.

Anodized: Coated with a protective oxide layer.

Antihalation: The bottom layer of a photopolymer plate intended to reduce the tendency of light to reflect in different directions from the support material.

Aperture: the transparent window of the imaging on the film negative.

Backward reading: The text or image are structurally reversed, as if seen in a mirror.

Barweld rule: A type of brass rule which can be used for printing, or as roller bearers on the press bed outside the print area.

Bitmap: The collection of individual dots, or pixels, that make up a screen image.

Boxcar base: The popular brand of ruled flatbases, manufactured by the supplier of photopolymer plates, and supplier of printing supplies of the same name.

Cat wink: Kinked areas of a film negative.

Density gain: Ink accumulation causing a thickening or distorting of letterform outline.

Die cutting: Involves the use of sharp steel rules or custom dies to cut a specific pattern into paper or other material.

DPI: Dots Per Inch; a measure of the resolution of a computer monitor, scanner, or other output device.

Drainage pattern: Areas of an image or text in which the impression well can be more or less pronounced depending on the length of exposure, such as the inside hemisphere of a lowercase *e*.

Drawsheet: Cylinder packing top blankets.

Dwell: The length of time the paper is in contact with the plate during printing.

Edition State: The optimal level of inking for uniform printing throughout an edition.

Embossing/debossing: A process in which images, patterns, or text are stamped or pressed into a printing surface.

Emulsion side: The surface of a photographic film to which the light-sensitive emulsion has been applied.

Flatbase: A flat surface used to mount a printing plate or type-form in letterpress printing.

Floor: The printing plate's antihalation layer.

Form: A page or assembly of pages that can be printed simultaneously in a single impression.

Frisket mask: A strong, protective paper used to cover any portion of a printing plate not intended to be printed.

Furniture: Wood or metal blocks used to fill the blank spaces in a form.

Ganging: Grouping images together when making negatives, rather than making each exposure separately.

Halftones: Any image that exists as a series of small dots of varying size and color density that serve to simulate the appearance of continuous gradations of tone as in photographs.

Hardness readings: The durometer or hardness measurement of a polymer printing plate is a product of the raw plate stock chosen. It directly impacts ink acceptance and transfer, and print characteristics of the plate. Also used to describe the surface properties of printing press rollers and cylinders.

Image gain: Ink spread beyond letterforms due to overinking or bad presswork; or during the transition from digital type to negative to photopolymer plate, the tendency of letterforms to thicken. See chapters 17 and 20.

Impression: The pressure necessary to transfer a printed image from a printing plate, blanket, or other image carrier to the paper or other substrate.

Ink acceptance: The characteristic of the printing area of the surface of a polymer or other printing plate to accept (or reject) ink. High acceptance is desirable.

Ink transfer: The characteristic of the printing area of the surface of a polymer or other printing plate to transfer ink to paper during printing.

Interpolating: Interpolation is the creation of an intermediate font from two related fonts within a digital type family.

Kerning: The reduction of letter-spacing between certain characters or punctuation performed for aesthetic reasons.

Key: Small metal tool used to lock or unlock quoins.

Kreene: A flexible, transparent plastic sheeting used in platemakers on vacuum tables for a tight seal over film and plate.

LPI: Lines Per Inch. A measurement of resolution for halftone images, defining how close together the lines in a halftone grid are.

Makeready: Collective term for both the process and materials associated with seting up a printing press prior to printing (specific to a particular job and its ink, paper, and type or plates).

Matrix case: The holder for the 225 (later 272) individual character matrices which make up a font for a Monotype type caster.

Monotype composition machine: A mechanized typecasting device that enabled a keyboard operator to set type by punching holes in a paper ribbon, which then triggers the casting of individual letters by a casting machine.

Mouldmade paper: A machine made paper with some of the content, surface and edge textures and features characteristic of handmade paper.

Out of sorts: A sort is a piece of type representing a single letter or symbol. Hence the phrase of "out of sorts" is used to refer to being short the requisite number of sorts to finish a printed piece.

Pin registration: The use of pins to provide precise registration in relief printing.

Platen press: A configuration of printing press that presses a flat inked typeform, plate, or cutting die onto a flat sheet of paper or other material.

Plate travel: Movement of a printing plate out of register.

Point size: A measure of the height of the capitol characters of a font measured in points.

Proof: Any early or singular copy produced as a means of checking for typos or similar errors in images.

Quoin: A wooden or metal wedge used to secure type in the frame after hand tightening.

Registration: Alignment of printing plates with each other and the paper (as presented by the cylinder), resulting in proper positioning of text and image on the printed page.

Reglets: Wood spacing material used to provide space between lines of type, or as spacing material for large wood type.

Repro proof: One of the purposes for which cylinder proof presses were created was the production of single, perfect impressions of metal type, used in prepress for production printing.

Shear strength: The resistance to side-to-side stress.

Substrate: Term for any surface to be printed to which ink will adhere, primarily paper.

Tolerance: The acceptable amount of variance from stated specifications.

Tracking: The adjusting of the letter-spacing throughout a piece of typeset copy. Not to be confused with kerning, which modifies spacing between individual letter or character pairs.

Tympan: A hard, generally coated paper used on letterpress printing presses as a means of packing—or adjusting the height of—the image carrying surface.

Type High: The distance from the foot to the printing face of a type character, in America .918 inches.

Underlay: A sheet of paper or other material used to increase the height of a printing plate, flatbase, or form.

Undersheet: A sheet paper or other material used to increase the height of the printing plate.

Under blanket: A sheet of paper, rubber, or other material used to increase the height of the tympan.

Workup: With metal type, letters and spacing material can work their way up during printing, high enough to hit both ink rollers and paper. Except for problems caused by poor lockup, this is generally more of an issue with printing from metal type than from photopolymer plates.